Praise for
Choose Trust

"A must-read for anyone in an educational environment looking to foster trust and collaboration."

> **—Diane O'Dowd, professor emerita,**
> **University of California at Irvine**

"An excellent guide to help you navigate the waters of collaboration and trust in business. A survival manual for the twenty-first century."

> **—John Philpin, founder, People First,**
> **and former CEO of Lyris**

"Thought-provoking and full of common sense from start to finish, in addition to being an excellent reference for practical situations."

> **—Mark Harvey, CFO, Gen Phoenix**

"Unlike so many books on this subject, *Choose Trust* looks at the challenges and opportunities of trust from multiple angles, with practical, real-world insights to transform the way you operate at work."

> **—Charles H. Green, co-author of**
> ***The Trusted Advisor***

"A brilliant read from genuine experts on relationship building. The thinking around trust-based leadership and teamwork is thought-provoking—lessons that would benefit many in modern business."

> **—Steve Cullen, founding partner, Merlin5**

Choose Trust

Building Relationships for Business Success

Stuart Maister and Kevin Vaughan-Smith

The Economist

CHOOSE TRUST

Published with permission from *The Economist* by Pegasus Books.

The Economist is an imprint of
Pegasus Books, Ltd.
148 West 37th Street, 13th Floor
New York, NY 10018

First Pegasus Books cloth edition February 2025

ISBN: 978-1-63936-817-4

10 9 8 7 6 5 4 3 2 1

Printed in the United States of America
Distributed by Simon & Schuster
www.pegasusbooks.com

PEGASUS BOOKS
NEW YORK LONDON

Stuart: to my children and close friends

Kevin: to Hayley, Mia, Anya and Carys – the support of my family makes the difference

Also in the Economist Edge series

Branding That Means Business
by Matt Johnson and Tessa Misiaszek

Innovating with Impact
by Ted Ladd and Alessandro Lanteri

Giving Good Feedback
by Margaret Cheng

Best Story Wins: Storytelling for business success
by Mark Edwards

Influence at Work
by Steve Martin

The Power of Culture
by Laura Hamill

About the authors

Stuart Maister

After a ten-year career as a national TV and radio reporter for the BBC, ITN and Sky, Stuart has worked at the most senior level with businesses and public organisations as a consultant, coach, trainer and producer. He has led four different companies, selling his first award-winning business to a NASDAQ-listed firm and running all their international operations.

He has focused his work on the areas of storytelling and trust building. His mission is to help people and businesses articulate their truths and live by them in the way they engage with others in their work.

Stuart developed the concept of the Strategic Narrative, the articulation of the organisation or individual's value proposition and approach to the marketplace, focusing on areas of greatness and using this to drive strategy. Together with Kevin Vaughan-Smith he founded Mutual Value Ltd, a business based on changing the behaviours around leadership and sales to focus on trust building, not transaction.

Stuart has two children and lives in Brighton, in the south of England.

Kevin Vaughan-Smith

Kevin spent twenty years with IT companies such as IBM and Digital Equipment, where he built a reputation for creating large-scale client relationships and award-winning teams, including nine years leading Digital Equipment to no. 2 supplier to the UK government. He then transitioned to sharing his expertise in relationship building and leadership by establishing his own consulting business before being invited to take over at Franklin Covey as MD in the UK. He continued to focus on working with large clients in leadership, team building and client engagement before joining EY as an associate partner responsible for changing the go-to-market approach of its 16,000 employees.

On leaving EY, Kevin and Stuart joined forces to continue to promote the importance of trust and trustworthiness through their business Mutual Value Ltd.

Kevin lives on the edge of England's Chiltern Hills with his wife Hayley, a highly respected counsellor and psychology content writer. They have three children.

Contents

Introduction: why choose trust?

In 2021, the price of the digital currency Bitcoin soared to a record high of $69,000, a rise of seven times its value over 12 months. Cryptocurrency was enjoying a surge. It had suddenly become a popular way for people to speculate and even trade.

Despite many warnings about the dangers involved, millions of people were beginning to engage with crypto. Major banking institutions were investing their clients' funds, and there were many stories of crypto millionaires, with a lot of speculation about major growth to come.

At the centre of this whole story was the development and maintenance of widespread trust in this new, exciting system. It's the foundation of everything you do too, as this book will show.

Perhaps a backlash was inevitable. International financial institutions were nervous. Debates raged about whether this was a real revolution in money and payments or simply a set of scams. Some countries, like the UK, blacklisted exchanges that people were using to buy and sell crypto.

By June 2022, the price of Bitcoin had plummeted to below $18,000. A major cryptocurrency lending company announced that it was freezing withdrawals and transfers because of "extreme" conditions. Cryptocurrency exchange Binance paused Bitcoin withdrawals because of a "stuck transaction" that was causing a backlog.

Trust in this amazing new source of value was reducing rapidly.

Then, in November 2022, it was dealt an even heavier blow. A major cryptocurrency exchange, FTX, went out of business after Binance pulled out of a deal to buy it. At the start of 2022, FTX was valued at $32bn. By the end of the year, it was worthless.

Worse, the practices revealed by its bankruptcy suggested there was fraud and perhaps even criminality involved, which caused speculation about whether this was true across the crypto world. The whole edifice of crypto was based on one thing: trust. And when that was damaged, its value crashed.

This may be an extreme example of an industry with no product and value created by pure speculation. But the fact is that at the base of every organisation is the trust that people place in it. From the smallest sole trader to the biggest companies, not to mention governments, institutions and entire nations, this trust underpins how they engage with everyone and everything. It's that big. When trust disappears or is damaged, behaviours change.

There's one simple reason for this. The power of choice.

People who buy from you, sell to you, work with or for you, or decide whether to employ you, have choice. They are selecting from a number of options. Even those who *have to* deal with you will decide whether to put in discretionary effort to do more, or simply transact.

The simple fact is: people choose positively when they trust and are trusted. This powerful idea can change everything about how you engage with others in your working life.

Choosing trust

When a small child looks at their parents, their love is based on total trust. It's an instinct that's never lost. If you consider your own most important relationships – partner, friend, relative – which are the best ones? And what makes them so?

You want the best for each other.

This is an innate need from birth. People want to bond with others they can relate to and can rely on. For this to be true, they need to be able to trust those people too.

It's easy to forget that these truths apply just as much in the world of work. Organisations are made up of human beings who have relationships with each other. Turning this simple idea into a strategy can give you a competitive edge.

You may choose a supplier, colleague, partner or even who you work for because of a range of factors, but the people you stick with tend to be the ones you trust. Yet, at work, it's easy to forget this, to focus on other things or to feel the need to "be professional" or "to perform". This can lead to behaviours that damage, rather than build, trust.

The central message of this book is that the most professional and effective way to behave at work is to trust and to be trustworthy. This is the way to build better relationships which create far more value for everyone involved. It can affect every conversation, every meeting, every time you deliver a presentation, create a proposal or respond to an email.

The difference at work is that you need to develop this habit *deliberately*. Intentionally. Consciously. This needs a structured approach. That's what this book will provide. It will show you how to apply some key principles, whether you're leading or selling, collaborating or partnering. Being trustworthy and intentional about building trusting relationships is a powerful way to position yourself and, ultimately, your organisation.

The book offers a structure and detailed thinking about every aspect of trust that is applicable whatever you do and wherever you work.

In more formal situations – such as managing a major contract or building a team – it is worth going through each of the exercises and thinking through all the dimensions of trust to build a much more solid foundation for your relationships. Many of the ideas and exercises will be a great basis for a workshop or discussion.

On a day-to-day basis, where there is a need or desire to build trust with other people quickly, you may find that one or two of the ideas here will resonate with you, and that different ideas will hit home in different situations.

In *all* situations you will find it valuable to consider why deliberately building trust is such a critical aspect of the way you interact with others, and to have ways of doing so that you can reach for quickly and easily.

Technology is changing the world at a breathtaking pace. Artificial intelligence promises to bring huge benefits and potential threats. Social media can manipulate, and some has malign intention. What this world increasingly does is make us less and less connected to other human beings, with machines operating according to set rules with no discretion or judgement. This is perhaps the biggest driver of a general distrust which all research suggests widely exists. In such an environment, being more human can be a major advantage. Focus on this innate human urge to trust others and be trusted so that, when choices are made, people decide to work with you.

The founder of eBay, Pierre Omidyar, says that the company's business is based on "enabling someone to do business with another person, and to do that, they first have to develop some measure of trust, either in the other person or the system". What he describes is a principle that can be applied by people working in all types and sizes of organisation.

In your next meeting, or your next conversation, actively choosing high-trust behaviour could radically change the outcome. A deliberate focus on building and preserving trust as a central part of your approach to others can make the difference between success and failure.

Defining trust

What is trust?

Many people see trust as an instinctive thing: "I know when I can trust someone." It's seen as something indefinable, that's felt rather than seen. The problem with this is that it is impossible to bake feelings into your personal strategy or company culture or measure its impact. It cannot just be something individuals generate if it's to be a consistent deliverer of value. Otherwise people shrug their shoulders and say that some have trust and some don't.

We believe that trust is based on three dimensions: clarity, character and capability. These are all interdependent if trust is to be earned and given in a relationship.

These dimensions form our trust triangle. They provide the foundation for the practical approaches set out in this book.

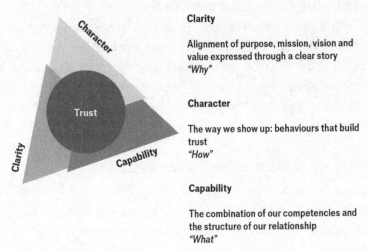

Clarity

Alignment of purpose, mission, vision and value expressed through a clear story
"Why"

Character

The way we show up: behaviours that build trust
"How"

Capability

The combination of our competencies and the structure of our relationship
"What"

Figure 1: **The trust triangle**

The triangle serves as a design principle for the relationships you want to build and grow in your working life.

It's not the first time there has been an attempt to define trust in business, but this book contains three departures from previous approaches.

External vs internal focus

Books on trust often focus on how to become *trustworthy* to achieve an outcome – for example, to gain the trust of a customer. It's an important but essentially internally focused approach, intended to create a win for the person using it. By contrast, this book will focus on the *relationships* you want to create, with an emphasis on this being a two-way street, with value created for everyone involved.

What you'll learn here can work as a tool to ensure that you (and, through its people, your organisation) are consistently trustworthy. That is highly valuable. But even greater results can be achieved if you use the tools as a way of building a trusting relationship with others to *co-create* value together.

In almost all situations there is interdependence, which means that all sides need to trust each other for the best relationships to be established. The trust triangle provides the vocabulary to agree the basis of trust between everyone involved, and how they will be held accountable for acting accordingly.

The need for accountability and consequences

Most approaches to trust fall down in one key area: the transition from warm words to actual, consistent behaviours. Where there is an intention to create a trusting relationship together, it is important to agree both the accountability and the consequences if those involved depart from the agreed behaviours, including a process for regular review. This is what gives this approach teeth and encourages difficult, honest discussions about what can go wrong – as well as enthusiastic, optimistic dialogue, which often characterises the beginning of a relationship.

The start of a work relationship can be like a wedding. When you win that contract, or join a new company, agree a new partnership, become a new leader, it's as if everyone is in love. There is no shortage of huge, positive statements of intent.

But the real work is in the marriage. Months later there are problems, difficulties – the professional equivalent of the baby crying at 3am. If there is no real commitment to the relationship, trust is destroyed. This book helps you address that so that you can maintain the same spirit that characterised the relationship at the outset.

A focus on clarity

The third differentiator is an emphasis on the foundation element of the three dimensions in the trust triangle: clarity. It's foundational because misunderstanding is so often the cause of mistrust, simply because those involved had different expectations or interpret what others have done through a different lens. The more you are clear about and align expectations and achieve mutual understanding, the higher the levels of trust.

The three dimensions of the trust triangle

Clarity: the why

Have you ever completed a project knowing that you have done a great job, but then discover that your customer or colleague is unhappy because it wasn't what they were expecting? Have you ever commissioned work only to find out that the person responsible is not carrying it out as you wanted them to, or as you would have done yourself? Or perhaps that a supplier has done the work but is charging you more than you had anticipated?

When this happens, trust is destroyed. Being clear together, making sure everyone involved has the same ambition for the work together, is the critical foundation for trust.

The book will demonstrate the impact of a lack of clarity – and how to create more clarity in the first place.

Character: the how

This is the dimension that addresses the behaviours that need to be demonstrated consistently by those involved in the relationship. It's important to decide the behaviours expected of all parties deliberately and collectively, to look at what this means in practice, and to hold each other accountable for them.

Once again, the behaviours involved are the ones agreed as appropriate by those in the relationship. You may regard the way you engage with others as entirely reasonable. They may see things differently. In this gap, trust is destroyed.

The approaches set out in the book will help you to consciously decide the right behaviours and apply them in practical ways – for example, in meetings and conversations.

Capability: the what

A key component of trust is to do what you say you will do when you say you will do it, and on the basis you agreed. However, this ignores the fact that, in many cases, your ability to do this is affected by the capability of the person you're interacting with; your customer, partner, colleague or employer also needs to play their part. This *interdependence* is a key component of capability, and is either the foundation or the destroyer of a sustainable, trusting relationship.

The question is this: are those involved capable of behaving in a trustworthy, collaborative manner with each other? Are they clear about the structure of the relationship? Establishing this, and setting up ways to maintain the ambition and behaviours that build trust, is the secret to having a powerful trust capability. The book explores what this means in practice and how to make sure this capability is in place.

The interdependence of the three Cs

Each of these three dimensions – clarity, character and capability – will be considered in turn. However, all three need to work together to build high-trust relationships that create value.

You may be clear about what you plan to do with someone else, so you have achieved *clarity*. But if you then behave in ways that destroy trust (*character*) or together you fail to demonstrate the *capability* to work collaboratively, trust is damaged.

You may do a great job for your customer – demonstrating your *capability* – but that doesn't mean there was *clarity* about what you were meant to do. The result may be that you disappointed the customer in some way, which causes them to start to doubt your *capability* and behave accordingly, so they lose trust in you and doubt your *character.*

You may behave in very high-trust ways, demonstrating great *character*, but without *clarity* about what you are doing together or the *capability* to do so, trust will be damaged.

If not properly nurtured and agreed, any one of the three dimensions of the trust triangle can damage or destroy trust. Trust is a fragile flower which can be crushed much more easily than it can be nurtured. That's why it is so important to look to build trust intentionally.

The interdependence of the parties involved

You can use every method in this book to become more trustworthy.

But real trust is a two-way street. In most situations where you create value, you do it *with* people, not *for* them. That's why the most effective way to choose trust is to be clear about the interdependence of everyone involved and make that a powerful, sleek engine of value creation, not a complex system that gets in the way. You can use the trust triangle with others to choose trust together.

Even in a situation where you are providing a product or service to others – customers or colleagues – the effectiveness of what you provide depends to some degree on the way it is received or used. Other people's behaviours may be a factor in the value you create for them. That's why interdependence is so important and why trust is the basis of a relationship, not simply a virtue. It's also why the trust triangle provides a framework for consciously designing working relationships that last, even when things go wrong.

Everyone wants to trust those they work with and for. And, in a world where trust is often considered to be in short supply, being the leader, seller, buyer, colleague or partner who gives and receives trust will give you a major advantage.

In routine interactions, it means things work better. In bigger, more formal relationships, it means you win and continue to win together. In all types of ways in which you work with others, it means people make a positive choice in ways that benefit you: they choose you as a supplier or employer; they do extra discretionary work as a team member or partner; you have more influence as a colleague or fellow leader.

The key is for you to choose trust and know what to do about it.

How to use this book

This book is designed to provide you with a simple framework to use to build and maintain trust, and then looks in detail at how this shows up in specific working situations. The ideas here are intended to inspire you to consider how they apply in your working world, and give you practical ways to use them.

Each chapter sets out some key questions you can ask yourself to explore your own behaviours and those of the people around you. Chapters also contain practical exercises you can do on your own, with a team and with customers and clients to help build trust into your working life. They are designed to help you explore issues in a structured way.

Part 1 sets out the choice between having a transactional mindset or a trust mindset. Chapter 1 considers why being transactional has become the default in many work situations and the negative impact it has. Chapter 2 sets out the case for the opposite – the trust mindset. It will explore the difference it makes if you choose trust as a key strategy, whether as an individual or an organisation, and how this creates far greater value for everyone involved.

Part 2 dives into the trust triangle and looks in detail at each of the three dimensions. Chapter 3 focuses on clarity, the foundation of trust. It explores what happens when there's a lack of clarity and sets out a simple approach to being clear. Chapter 4, on character, sets out five principles of behaviour that can serve as a useful framework to explore real-life situations and how they can be tackled in a high-trust way. Chapter 5 puts some teeth into the process, asking you to ground things in a clear analysis of your capabilities both in terms of your interdependence and the way you govern the relationship.

Part 3 shows what this can look like in practice. In each case the trust triangle is the framework that underpins the approach. You may choose to go straight to the chapter which most directly reflects your own situation or current focus. Chapter 6 sets out an approach to high-trust leadership that will ask you to consider what great, trusting leadership looks like, and how leaders can destroy trust if they are not intentional about this. Chapter 7 explores how you can build more successful teams using the approaches in this book, and contrasts this with the situation when people are really working as a group rather than as a team.

Chapter 8 tackles business development. Building trust with customers and clients is the only way to ensure loyalty and growth. This chapter focuses on when the engagement is in person, rather than mass marketing, but many of the principles apply in all contexts.

Chapter 9 looks at trust in how you work with your suppliers: how you create trust as a buyer of goods and services and why this is a more successful way to do business. The chapter sets out a philosophy which turns into a practical way to engage with your suppliers and partners that can change the whole tenor of your work together.

In every relationship, meetings and discussions are where trust is most often built or destroyed, and so in Chapter 10 we offer a structured approach to conversations which, if followed, will mean you are always building trust, even if the subject matter is difficult.

This book is based on a clear philosophy. You have a choice in your working life between being highly transactional or highly trustworthy. In fact, almost no one wants to see themselves as untrustworthy; few people go to work aiming simply to transact. But they do not choose to put this at the centre of their thinking. The results can be seen through some of the examples you will read here.

You probably regard yourself as highly trustworthy. This book will ask you to analyse your actions and behaviours to see if they create or destroy trust, usually inadvertently. It will encourage you to test with colleagues whether or not they feel they can trust you and, if they can, to ask why. If you can seek this feedback with genuine inquiry, it will help you discover more about your relationships.

If you choose trust in an intentional way, it's a much more enjoyable and rewarding way to work, because it creates better relationships. People will know they can rely on what you say, and you will create far greater value for yourself and those around you.

PART 1

Why trust matters

It seems obvious that trust is important, but most of us casually destroy it every day in our professional lives through ingrained behaviours and structures. This is rarely deliberate. It's just that, when you think about how you do things at work, often your actions and behaviours are not designed to create trust but simply to achieve an outcome.

When you consider how others work with you – as colleagues, leaders or people who want to sell you something – this may become even more clear. Part 1 of this book is intended to get you into a total trust mindset, ready to explore what this looks like in practice in Parts 2 and 3.

Chapter 1 sets out what destroys trust – the transactional mindset. This chapter will look at why this has become the default in many work situations and the negative impact it has. From the collapse of a global accountancy firm to the sudden deregulation of the financial markets in what became known as the Big Bang, through the technology everyone used in the time of covid, the trend is towards a more transactional mindset.

Chapter 2 sets out what creates trust – the trust mindset. This chapter will explore the difference it makes if you choose trust as a key strategy, whether as an individual or an organisation, and looks at why and how this creates far greater value for everyone involved.

In each chapter we will set out some key questions you should ask yourself to explore how true this is in your own behaviours and those of the people around you.

1

The power of trust – and why most people don't choose it

> "A man who trusts nobody is apt to be
> the kind of man nobody trusts."
>
> *Harold Macmillan, British prime minister*

In 2002, after 89 years in business, Arthur Andersen ceased to be an auditor. Before it became embroiled in a major scandal involving the energy firm Enron, it had 28,000 US employees. By the time it was forced to relinquish or revoke its licences to operate, the number of employees was down to 3,000.

The company, one of the Big Five global accountancy firms, collapsed in a matter of months. Accusations that it had turned a blind eye to the Enron leadership's accounting fraud, and then obstructed justice by shredding documents, created too big a scandal for the company to survive.

In fact, this conviction was reversed, and only a tiny proportion of Arthur Andersen employees was involved. But the damage had been done. The reputation of the whole organisation was in tatters. Despite its huge global presence, a giant of the financial system collapsed all too quickly once it lost its most important asset: *trust*.

The company had always stood for ethics and honesty. Its founder, Arthur Andersen, originally built the business "by putting reputation over profit". So what had changed?

An article in the *Wall Street Journal* summed it up like this.

> Andersen leaders responded [to pressure to perform] by pushing partners to become salesmen – upsetting the delicate balancing act any auditor must perform between pleasing a customer and looking out for the public investor.[1]

It's an extreme reminder that trust is the basis of all relationships, at work as well as in life. In the pursuit of immediate profit, the individuals at Arthur Andersen had been encouraged to act in ways that compromised relationships based on trust. The cumulative effect was enough to bring down an entire organisation.

Once you no longer trust someone or something, you lack confidence that any promise they make will be kept. If they appear untrustworthy, you avoid them. When you have a choice, you look elsewhere for the service they provide. Or, if you have to deal with them, you do so in a very transactional way, checking everything and only giving what you have to so that you get what you need or want.

The *Collins Dictionary* defines trust in a helpful way, through a series of sentences.

- If you **trust** someone **to** do something, you believe that they will do it.
- Your **trust in** someone is your belief that they are honest and sincere and will not do anything to harm you.
- If you **trust** someone's judgement or advice, you believe that it is good or right.
- If you say you **trust that** something is true, you mean you hope and expect that it is true.

For most people, this is a simple statement of how you want to be seen by others. In your working life, it is important that, to a greater or lesser degree, these statements are true about you. And it's important that you see others with whom you work in the same way.

Consider the opposite of all these sentences. Replace "trust" with "do not trust" and think about the opposite of what you expect or believe as a result. Where this is true, it is deadly to commercial and professional relationships. Here's what it looks like.

- If you **do not trust** someone to do something, you believe that they will *not* do it.

- Your **distrust** in someone is your belief that they are *not* honest and sincere and *may do something* to harm you.

- If you **do not trust** someone's judgement or advice, you believe that it is *not* good or right.

- If you say you **do not trust that** something is true, you mean you *do not* hope and expect that it is true.

Most people would not want anyone to say any of this about themselves. And yet this crucial factor is often overlooked in the way people work together. They focus instead on what is to be done, how much it will cost and how well the work will be carried out.

Entire countries suffer when outside investors no longer trust the actions of the government. That corner store you went to suffers if something happens that causes you not to trust the goods it sells or the manner in which it sells them – and so you no longer choose to shop there. At the most personal level, if someone betrays your trust, then whatever joy you created together will not be repeated.

Exercise: Who do you trust, why, and what impact does it have?

Think about who you do *not* trust.

Is there an organisation or person you deal with only grudgingly, or simply because it is convenient or necessary to do so? If so, think about what they have done – or not done – to put you in this frame of mind when dealing with them.

It may be a landlord, a colleague or boss, a company you buy goods from, a utility, a shop. What did they do? How do you behave when dealing with them? Consider the impact this has on your willingness to do anything for them that involves some discretionary behaviour on your part.

For example, if this is your boss, will you go the extra mile when asked? If it is a company, how do you feel when you pay them? Do you resent it or are you happy to pay for the service or goods provided?

And, if you were that person or organisation, is that how you would want your customers, colleagues or investors to feel about you? Think about the value that is destroyed when this situation exists, when there is no trust, simply a transaction.

Now think about who you *do* trust.

Consider someone or an organisation or company you trust. How does your behaviour differ? What have they done – or not done – to make you behave in this way? Would you want others to feel that way about you? Would you choose to deal with others who give you this level of confidence?

Think about the difference.

That difference is the outcome of trust, whether it is present or absent. It is inconceivable that you would choose for others not to trust you, your team or organisation. Yet you will have thought about people or companies that destroy trust daily, and it is probably true that, if asked, they would say the same as you. They think they're trustworthy. Yet you don't trust them.

When you do this exercise, you may find that the central reason that trust does not exist is when your relationship or engagement with others is *transactional* in nature: the person or organisation deals with you in a way that is functional and focused on what you do for them, and what they do for you. It may be that what you do is simply to hand over cash in return for a product or service, or vice versa – for example, your employer paying you for your work.

If trust does not exist, then you will continue to take the money until you get a better job. You will calculate the value of the transaction and continue until there is a better one. Your employer may do the same: keep paying you until they no longer see value in keeping you. And you know that is the case, so you do not trust them.

Similarly, you will continue to go to that shop until you see a better option. Where you have discretion, you will use it to change without thinking twice. Compare that with shopping at a place where you really believe in the good intentions of those selling to you, and the experience is a good one. That's a relationship you'd be sorry to lose, to the extent that you might be less price conscious as a result.

This leads to the question: do you really know how much others trust you or your organisation?

Once, when the village was the typical place to live and its inhabitants worked and shopped locally, every person had to protect their reputation because they lived with the consequences of any betrayal of trust for the rest of their lives. The world today is very different, and many of the factors that have led to a highly transactional mindset are relatively recent.

How did we get here?

"My word is my bond." This remains the motto of the London Stock Exchange, but the idea on which it is based was swept away in October 1986. The Big Bang in the City of London changed the rules about who could or could not trade stocks and shares in London, and led to a wave of takeovers and mergers, many involving overseas banks, that swept aside a culture that had developed over centuries.

In the old world, personal relationships between brokers and jobbers were key. Trust was critical to the system, and without it you could not do your job. After 1986 the move towards a highly transactional, impersonal trading system was inexorable and personal trust was no longer a major factor in success.[2]

The Big Bang paved the way for new digital trading and provided the foundation for a boom in fast-paced transactions that have accelerated, driving stocks up and down at a new pace. Those running listed companies continually focus on volatile stock prices, a system which rewards short-term decision making and eye-catching initiatives that may be attractive to transactional investors but can destroy trust among customers, employees and partners.

It's a story that is reflected in the way businesses are financed across the world, however they are set up. The pressure to perform quickly and demonstrate continual growth has led to an increasing focus on short-term results and transactional behaviour.

Such specialisation and the drive for efficiency has its roots in the Industrial Revolution. Instead of small local firms doing everything, larger businesses grew up which focused on one thing and did it brilliantly. This division of labour, international trading and empire-building led to complex supply chains where the users of a product or service had little or nothing to do with the people who contributed to its creation.

In the professions – accountants, lawyers, engineers, architects – new firms were founded by experts who recruited like-minded people and built their success on selling that expertise into the market. It's been a story of success that has a history of over 150 years based on building into the system the idea that expertise can be traded as a commodity like any other.

As organisations grew bigger, they became less personal. The relationships of trust that were critical to a small marketplace got lost in the drive for growth, expansion and financial success. The rise of the joint stock company – the basis of every limited and listed business today – meant that investors too were no longer directly connected to the firms in which they invested, and vice versa. Stock in a company became itself a commodity to be traded, its value varying depending on many different factors, not all related to the fundamental performance of the business.

Yet as recently as the first half of the 20th century many businesses still behaved according to a strong ethical base. They were led by their founders and underpinned by the strong personal connections that remained a feature of most commercial activity, which largely remained local in nature.

Hyper-globalisation after the Second World War began to loosen the ties. Technology ripped them apart. The impersonal trading that took over stock exchanges was mirrored by the systemisation of every aspect of business. In the digital world the numbers are what count, and this drives behaviours and intent in every aspect of our working lives.

Covid accelerated history to the world of Zoom, Teams and Google Hangouts. Initially, many people felt it was great that they could see into each other's front rooms – wasn't this personalising business again? But the reality is that this means of connecting moves us even further into a transactional world where every conversation has a purpose and participants take it in turns to speak. Now there are fewer "water cooler moments" that result in human-to-human, casual conversations.

The result of all this? Many of your customers, employees, colleagues and teams feel disconnected. They view you, your company, its products and services, and their connection with it, as a transaction that they continue while it serves them. And you may view them in the same way.

As you will see, this leads to bad leadership, salespersonship, colleagueship and partnership. It results in poorer service and much lower value creation. But it also creates an opportunity for people and organisations who go in exactly the opposite direction of travel: to focus instead on building trust, to behave in ways that demonstrate that and be rewarded by the value created because they are trusted and more able to trust those with whom they work.

This somehow feels like an old-fashioned concept, dating back to those days when we were all local and accountable to our neighbours. It is. And yet it is also a totally modern idea because consumers, employees and colleagues are becoming alienated from low-trust engagement and increasingly choosing to spend their time and money where they feel higher levels of trust, purpose and integrity.

The destruction of value: the transactional mindset

Time and again in the world of work, trust is damaged by this transactional mindset. It's an approach that focuses on the "facts": the numbers, the deal, the contract, what one person is buying and the other selling, whether that is a consumer item or service or their labour and time.

To trust is a fundamentally human-to-human emotion which was once the foundation of all commerce. But the way in which businesses are now measured and controlled puts pressure on everyone to focus on transactions.

From the earliest ledgers to the most recent complex accounting systems, success is judged by a list of inputs (costs) and outputs (revenue), and success is based on the difference between the two. Business is analysed down to the transaction – the focus is on deals, not customer relationships, profit per month, quarter or year, not employee or customer lifetime engagement. If you are a listed company you are judged by the daily stock price and its trend, not the success of your vision.

Under pressure, companies seldom, if ever, reflect on their vision or their strategy. They revert to age-old donkey leadership (carrot and stick) focus on cost reduction and squeezing the assets (mostly people) and respond by analysing how they can carry out more transactions at lower cost. And when they are successful, what is rewarded most often are the biggest transactions rather than the biggest contribution to the overall vision.

It's therefore no surprise that the people within this system are led to think and behave transactionally. They focus first on their own success, not that of the broader team, and not that of their customers and clients. In low-trust, transactional situations like this, collaboration is difficult even within teams, let alone beyond them.

Does that sound familiar? Just by recognising it you can probably immediately see the difficulties that result. But let's look at this in more detail.

The impact of a transactional mindset

In his book *The Speed of Trust*, Stephen Covey identifies that low trust has a very predictable outcome: that the speed of interaction falls and costs rise.[3] What does this mean in practice at work? As you read these examples, reflect on the extent to which they are familiar to you in your own experience.

Transactional leadership

You may have experienced low-trust leadership, sometimes called command and control. Despite many warm words by leaders to the contrary, some or all of these behaviours are still common.

Typically, low-trust leaders set goals and supervise based on lag measures – revenue, profit, costs. They don't create a compelling vision; they measure goal achievement and manage accordingly. Because of this, they take no responsibility for whether the goal is achievable, which means they cannot be clear on how these results should be achieved.

When things go wrong, you really see how low-trust leadership damages relationships. In an interview, Nicholas Hale, Group CEO of Movera (which dominates a specific area of property contract work in the UK), said:

> You're going to have stakeholders that pop up when everything's brilliant, they pop up in more voluminous ways when things are not going well, and they're silent in the middle. But if you really want to build trust, you need to be there through the whole journey.[4]

Hale has worked at various major companies in senior roles. He remembers one example where transactional leadership above him destroyed his trust in them because of how they behaved when he was facing a challenge. His team deployed a massive technology change. The new technology worked perfectly on 70 different sites, then, at the biggest location, which was processing 50,000 customer orders a day, someone flipped the button on a Monday morning. Everything stopped.

What followed was a demonstration of how not to lead. Hale found himself spending as much time managing upwards, to people who failed to fully trust him and his team, as he did sorting out the problem. As a result, the issue continued for three weeks. His conclusion is stark.

> In a bad moment, trust people more. Don't trust them less, because if you trust them less the impact on their ability to perform, their mental well-being, the way they show up and the way they implicitly cascade their behaviour onto the rest of the team is deeply unhelpful.

People at work often have choices. They expect leadership to be trusting and trustworthy, engaging, collaborative, giving them input to and ownership of the work they do. Many leaders aspire to this style of management but struggle to deliver.

Colleagues in low-trust environments

The psychologist B.F. Skinner is the person who coined the phrase "positive reinforcement". Considered the father of a psychological discipline called behaviourism, Skinner saw human actions as dependent on the consequences of previous actions. It now seems a simple idea: if the consequences of an action are bad, there is only a small chance that the action will be repeated; if the consequences are good, the probability of the action being repeated becomes higher.

In other words, human beings learn what happens when they act in a certain way and, if this is a positive experience, they do more of it. Think about how children are typically taught "right" and "wrong" behaviours. They are rewarded when they do the "right" thing and punished when they do the "wrong" thing.

At work, people learn quickly what is deemed right and wrong. If there is a win–lose culture based on top-down goals, carrot-and-stick leadership and transactional behaviour, these behaviours and culture will be replicated elsewhere. Even if colleagues like and trust each other on a personal level, they know that the expectation is that they should behave differently in a professional setting. Where transactional behaviour is encouraged and rewarded, the result is a culture based on low trust.

This shows up in familiar ways.

- Departments or individuals focus on achieving their own goals, whether that helps the organisation meet its vision or not – sometimes even at the cost of other people or teams. For example, salespeople complain that delivery teams don't build relationships for them to piggyback on; delivery people complain that what the salesperson has promised cannot be delivered, or at least delivered in a way that meets their cost and margin goals; someone overpromises to a customer and the team has to work harder to deliver on this.

- Different teams compete for scarce resources at budget time – often bidding for more than they need to make sure their needs are covered. Inevitably, in this win–lose environment, some teams will be under-resourced while others are in surplus, which reduces the likelihood of overall success.

- League tables celebrate "winners" and denigrate "losers" without any understanding of the complexity that may sit behind these simple numbers. The focus here is on competition, not collaboration, which is not an environment to create trust.

- Innovation is stifled because the high levels of openness and collaboration it requires is lacking. Innovation flourishes when people feel able to be vulnerable so that they can try new things and put forward ideas, comfortable that this will be welcomed. The opposite of a trust environment for innovation is a blame culture, where people feel inhibited about sharing new ideas and thinking in case things go wrong and they are stigmatised.

- People behave as though they are in a gig economy, selling their time to businesses transactionally. This can work in the short term but over a longer period it risks potential innovation, knowledge within the business and choice about who stays and who goes.

At its core, these are often symptoms of a failure to engage with a vision that creates a big picture that people understand. People "play narrow", focused on their targets or customers, with no reference to a broader ambition for the organisation.

Yet every organisation of every size has a stated ambition of being unified with the ability to take advantage of economies of scale across different departments and teams. This book will look at how to achieve this.

Transactional selling

There's someone at the door. When you answer it, it is clear he wants to sell to you. He tries to engage you in conversation, to connect, to explore your needs.

What is your reaction?

You will probably have a similar reaction to most people: you'll put up a barrier, make it difficult, resist and be suspicious, be on your guard. No one wants to be ripped off, and this is the danger that a salesperson represents.

In response, salespeople develop ever more sophisticated tactics. They learn clever sales techniques, find a way to grab your attention, maybe even exaggerate the benefits of what they are selling to get the sale.

What should be an exchange of value becomes a battle of

wits, with the walls between the parties getting higher and higher. Even large companies with major needs deliberately make it hard for people to sell to them and try to use procurement techniques to crush suppliers on cost. The incentive is to quote low and then ramp up prices when the job is won through change notices, new issues or add-ons.

Can you think of a more transactional situation than this? It is literally a transaction, and the result is that neither the buyer nor the seller gets the maximum value from the process. Trust is damaged and, instead of an open, collaborative approach to finding the best solutions, the parties focus on the deal or the sale. Often, this results in things going wrong when the product or service is delivered because the best solution was not chosen – and guess what happens? Trust is further damaged.

Yet many hold a belief about selling which is founded in a lack of trust, often compounded by tough targets to close deals. The result is that they focus on this more transactional mindset rather than on the fundamental needs of the customer.

This is a good moment to consider a fundamental idea. Figure 2 shows the belief model, which illustrates how what a person believes drives what they do and therefore the results they get. It shows why it's so hard to change ingrained thinking and behaviours.

If you want to change an outcome, it's tempting to focus on what people are doing – their actions. But that's not the place to start. What matters are the beliefs that drive what people do, and they can be limiting or empowering.

Whatever outcome is achieved usually serves to reinforce those beliefs, a process known as confirmation bias – the ability of the brain to give preference to data that supports its expectations, and to ignore contradictory evidence.[5]

If, in the case of selling, a buyer has the limiting *belief* that a

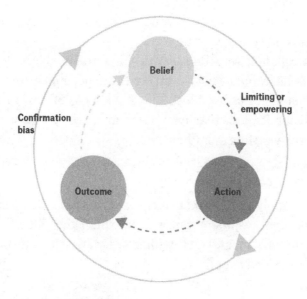

Figure 2: **The belief model**[6]

salesperson is untrustworthy, this leads to defensive behaviour. The *action* that results is that buyers restrict access, information flow and time to avoid being "sold to". This is true whether the purchase is a consumer item or a business deal.

By so doing they restrict the ability of the salesperson to really understand them or their business and they often get lower quality solutions than may have been available. That is the *outcome*.

Confirmation bias kicks in. The results reinforce their belief that they should not have trusted the sales process, and they raise barriers further. In large businesses this shows up as formalised procurement processes that are inappropriate for the acquisition of complex services and goods.

Salespeople, met with the barriers, driven by goals, take a self-interested approach to try to meet their own needs. By becoming self-serving and focused on the deal, they confirm the bias that buyers have – and so the transactional nature of buying and selling is reinforced.

Salespeople who transact will still sell, of course, reinforcing *their* beliefs about what works. But the opportunity to grow with the customer has been lost. This book looks at how to change the dynamic by embracing a different set of beliefs, with trust and trustworthiness at their core.

The transactional supply chain

Many supply chain arrangements founder, or at least produce sub-optimal results, because they exhibit the same low-trust behaviours that are seen within organisations and between customers and suppliers.

A supply chain is a combination of organisations providing products and services that together make up the final thing bought by the end user. Those in the supply chain are effectively the ingredients of the final product.

The successful outcome of this process depends on every link in the chain, so there is real interdependence between the different companies involved. But that is not how it can feel. More often, the primary company purchasing the services acts exactly like that – as a buyer – and so what they get in return is suppliers selling to them. Those transactional behaviours mean that both sides remain cautious and risk averse. They focus on the contract as the basis for how they work together.

The crazy thing is that the power balance often shifts once the purchase is made. The buyer becomes dependent on the seller to produce the final product or service, but if they have demonstrated a complete lack of trust at the purchasing stage, they will suffer the results in delivery.

Command and control contracting is the norm. The prime contractor or customer looks to maximise the value they generate from their suppliers by imposing tight restrictions, performance clauses and penalties for under-performance. They crush suppliers on cost.

One of the real failures of this approach is that suppliers are often hired in parallel, rather than in any collaborative process. They may then be expected to work together, or at least coordinate their activities, but have competing interests. In this situation, there is no incentive or mechanism for the different elements of the supply chain to collaborate. They may meet contractual obligations and, if the buyer has synchronised everything perfectly, this will work.

But then the real world intervenes. Something changes, or a link in the chain has difficulties, and this is the opportunity for one or more of the other suppliers to ask for more money or time because something happened that was not their fault.

In this situation, supply chains can demonstrate the worst of all the behaviours seen both internally and externally in organisations. Everyone in the chain is meant to be on the same side, producing an end-product or service, like colleagues in a single organisation. But when they are set up as transactions, they behave like distrustful buyers and sellers, focused on their own commercial interests. This creates vulnerability and far less value than would be the case if they collaborated and worked as a cohesive team, tackling issues together.

This book looks at how to create an alternative approach where sourcing suppliers is a far more effective process through adopting a high-trust approach to being a buyer.

Changing your mindset

This chapter has shown why and how trust can be so easily destroyed between buyers and sellers, leaders and the led, colleagues within organisations and suppliers and contractors.

The move from small, community-based commerce to national and global trade has led to technical specialism and a focus on transactions, rather than relationships, as the basis for the economy.

Yet in each specific situation this destroys value.

So what can you do about this? That is the subject of the rest of this book. Moving away from a transactional approach in business to trust-based relationships is not something that one can simply tell somebody to do. Everyone understands the importance of trust, but people often don't think to apply that knowledge in their day-to-day working lives. Building trust and trustworthiness takes work; you have to be intentional about it if you're going to challenge your own and others' beliefs and confirmation bias to change how you work.

And that's why the book now focuses on why and how you should consciously, intentionally and deliberately *choose* trust.

2

Choose trust to create more value

"He who does not trust enough will not be trusted."

Lao Tzu, Ancient Chinese philosopher and founder of philosophical Taoism

In the 1970s, the automotive sector in the UK was a byword for conflict and strife. Against that backdrop, John Neill took control of the British Leyland motor parts business and transformed it into Unipart, a firm focused on partnership and collaboration. A management buyout in 1987 began a journey that, decades later, sees Unipart as a global manufacturing, logistics and consulting business that operates across sectors.

The company has done this by implementing an approach it calls the Unipart Way. It's a philosophy and strategy based on building trust with employees, customers and its supply chain partners. Neill tells a powerful story of the way that Unipart partnered with Jaguar, then a Ford-owned company, to demonstrate how this has shaped its business.

Back in the early 1990s Jaguar had come to rely on Unipart for its spare parts in the UK, and together they had developed the first next-day delivery capability for its dealers. Uniquely, a Jaguar technician could order parts up to 6pm and expect next-morning delivery. But when Jaguar wanted to extend the service to France, neither Unipart nor Jaguar knew how they could service this very different market economically. That's when Neill and his counterpart at Jaguar, Nick Scheele, chose trust. They created a shared vision, setting themselves the target of matching the then world leader in supply chain logistics, Toyota, and achieving customer excellence for both Jaguar and its customers in France. This challenge was difficult for many reasons, but Neill was determined to demonstrate his firm's exceptional capabilities based on a real, collaborative team effort.

The most powerful demonstration of trust was that the only thing that Neill asked of Scheele was that they should cover his costs – which he would transparently share – and give him a reasonable margin. Asked by his worried finance team for details of how they would make money without formal contracts in place, his philosophy was: "I trust them. Why wouldn't they pay us if they are also getting good value?"

Quickly, two teams became one high-trust team and the operation in France expanded to cover Europe and then the world. This partnership has become so successful that it has lasted for decades, despite a change in Jaguar's ownership. Tens of millions of dollars of value have been created on a relationship in which trust was extended both ways.

If Chapter 1 suggests that business success has largely been achieved historically through a transactional mindset, this story illustrates a powerful alternative. In this and many other examples, the transactional mindset would have failed to maximise the potential when human beings come together with shared ambition and collaboration. This chapter explores what it takes to reach for that potential: a trust mindset.

If you take one thing from this book, it is in the title. Trust can develop by accident, but to be a real driver of value it needs to be something you consciously *choose* in your professional relationships. You need to develop your trust *mindset*.

Choosing trust starts with your intention. Here are four pillars that form the foundation of a trust mindset.

- I choose to be trustworthy.
- I choose to trust.
- I choose to build and maintain trust through active behaviour.
- I choose to adopt this approach with a fundamental belief that the benefits outweigh the effort needed to implement it.

These beliefs will drive you forward and help you to have the courage to operate with a win–win mindset over and above the transactional or win–lose thinking that is so often the norm.

The trust mindset is the reverse of the transactional mindset. As illustrated in Chapter 1, beliefs drive behaviours and so everything must start with the mindset of those who wish to trust and be trusted. But there is a fundamental challenge: if everyone else is thinking transactionally, can I really be different and succeed?

Ask yourself some simple questions.

- Do I want to be trusted and trustworthy?
- How would it feel if I could operate with customers, colleagues, suppliers, my boss, in a way that was more authentic to my nature?
- Would I perform better or worse?

Most people want to feel trusted and trustworthy. Indeed, many studies suggest that the quality of relationships in the workplace are increasingly important indicators as to whether employees feel engaged and give of their best.[1]

At the centre of this fact is the idea of psychological safety. Amy Edmondson, author of *The Fearless Organisation*, defines psychological safety in the workplace as: "the belief that one will not be punished or humiliated for speaking up with ideas, questions, concerns, or mistakes".[2] And Deloitte researched the impact of trust on overall company performance. It found that trusted companies outperform their peers by up to 400%.[3]

So perhaps what's important to consider is not: "Can I be different and succeed?" but rather: "How long can transactional thinking continue to be the standard approach?" Individuals who adopt the ideas in this book will find themselves at a competitive advantage. Instead of being "me too", where the value you create is the expertise you can apply to a transaction, your advantage can be the quality and depth of relationships you can repeatedly call upon to solve your most difficult issues and achieve your greatest goals.

It is worth exploring this in two areas.

The individual trust mindset

The chances are that you believe yourself to be trustworthy, or at least that you set out with that intent.

Here's a question for personal reflection.

When you're under pressure, do you tend to sacrifice a focus on trust and instead go for a short-term win? For example, do you feel under pressure to conform to others' views when they don't completely align with your values – for instance, to meet this quarter's numbers, or to give in to a demanding customer or supplier?

If your answer is "yes" to any of these, and you realise that you often do this, it is difficult to claim that you are trustworthy and reliable. You may well be giving in to the lure of transactional short-term thinking. And you wouldn't be alone. One of our clients defined a set of values, highlighting trust and trustworthiness as being central to their business, and then added the phrase "unless other commercial pressures apply".

Trust is simple to invoke, but takes real effort to demonstrate continually Take a long, hard look at your intentions in your role as an individual contributor, leader, salesperson, colleague or partner. Are those intentions focused on building trusted relationships and being trustworthy – or are they effectively self-oriented and transactional?

As a useful reference, let's use a model developed by management guru David Maister, known as the trust equation.[4]

$$\text{Trustworthiness} = \frac{\text{Credibility} + \text{Reliability} + \text{Intimacy}}{\text{Self-orientation}}$$

Figure 3: **The Maister trust equation**[5]

For Maister, trustworthiness is a combination of three key factors: credibility, reliability and intimacy. But he also identified an element that reduces trustworthiness, the divisor: self-orientation. Whatever you do or say, the degree to which you are doing so primarily to serve your own purposes reduces the likelihood that you will be trusted.

For example, it could be self-interest (and a desire to get a quick result) that causes you to go along with a colleague whose views you don't share (especially if they are the boss); to bow down to an angry customer or supplier; or to go for the quick win to meet your target, rather than pursue a better opportunity. All these are transactions that quickly teach your colleagues, customers and suppliers how to see you and how to get what they want in future.

What's lacking is a demonstration of the opposite of self-orientation: *other*-orientation. At the heart of the trust mindset is a willingness to consider the other party and to seek their success as much as your own. When that other party believes that you have their interests at heart, their behaviour towards you will change dramatically. This may lead you to challenge them, but to do so with the clear intent to achieve a better result together, rather than simply go with the flow.

In our experience what is often lacking is the courage to choose to be trustworthy. Too many people fear the consequences of being authentic to their values and even their ambitions. They worry that their boss won't be open to having their values or approach tested or challenged. They worry about how the customer might react if they want to move from a transactional to a more strategic relationship. What if the customer doesn't buy into the benefits or even the discussion? And many people who might lack the courage to be trustworthy are worried by the idea that, having made a mistake, they should take ownership of it. What might happen as a result?

How do you get the courage to choose trust? Here are a couple of ideas.

First ask yourself these two questions.

- How do I choose to react when others challenge my ideas or when I make a mistake?
- How do I feel if I don't achieve an agreed goal or target?

These are key trust opportunities. If in that moment you work collaboratively to understand what happened, correct a mistake and seek to learn or improve, you are extending trust and building a relationship that will perform better and better over time.

Second, use the belief model described in Chapter 1 (belief–action–outcome). This model reminds you that when people don't do what you might do, it's because they don't share your beliefs and so they get different results. If one of your colleagues or clients isn't getting a result you think they should be getting, or doing something you think they shouldn't be doing, have you sometimes thought: "What's wrong with those people? Are they stupid?"

Instead, try to understand how what *they* believe led to the actions that created a result you don't like. By doing this, you move from distrusting people towards understanding, being informed and being able to influence their thinking. This approach to working with others rapidly builds trust and gets to shared results far more effectively.

One of our clients experienced this with her marketing team. Faced with a new product launch, she expected the team to build a roadshow of events to share the new product with their channels. Historically, this approach had always been successful. But her team were reluctant to press ahead. Her frustration rising, she started to wonder if she had the right people on the project until she spoke to a senior team member. She asked: "Why aren't you doing what we have always done? That works."

She was surprised to be told: "The new marketing director doesn't see it that way. He believes we can achieve greater results by multi-touch marketing and webinars." Her beliefs were challenged. Fortunately, she chose to see this as an opportunity to gain new insight, and so she started to rebuild the trust that had been eroding.

Interestingly, the marketing director had clearly not taken the time to build trust in his methods with his colleague. In this case, neither leader saw trust as the starting point for collaboration and value creation, but instead viewed their role transactionally. One of them simply ordered a service; the other provided the service as they saw fit. Both were acting in good faith. Neither saw this as a relationship that needed to be nurtured. This is how mistrust develops, time is wasted and the best results are not achieved.

The courage to choose trust and be trustworthy flows from the experience of building trust quickly by taking simple steps like these. It is multiplied by the realisation that as soon as trust is extended to others, they tend to reciprocate. For example, think about when you have shared a problem with somebody: did they exploit your trust or respond positively? Most people will respond to your trust by being trustworthy. And this is an indicator of how trust builds trust far more quickly than many of us might believe.

Choosing to be transactional is often justified by short-term expediency. Have you ever heard (or said): "We just have to do it that way. That's what the customer wants and we need the revenue." This fails to demonstrate an ability to challenge clients and build trust through honesty.

This is a particular challenge for leaders. Employees learn more from what people do than from what they say, so it's critical that leaders demonstrate the value they place on trustworthiness and trust by choosing it, embodying it, discussing it, recognising it and rewarding it. Only when teams see it will they believe it. Conversely, when employees see a gap between the spoken word and action, they quickly learn what really matters.

One of the most common examples of the gap between words and behaviours is the way organisations describe their employees. How often have you heard these words: "Our people are our greatest asset"? Yet when the company comes under any pressure on its metrics, the first thing that is cut back is the investment in people: training stops, people are made redundant and pay rises are affected. This highlights a simple truth: that transactional leadership and accounting rules tell you that people are not an asset, they are an expense, and the easiest expense to reduce. Once these beliefs drive the actions of leaders, trust in what they say to the contrary disappears.

Exercise: Adopting the trust mindset

It's a good start to want to be trustworthy and trusted, and there are also some great ways to enhance that decision and help you turn your choice into reality. Here's a roadmap that will give you confidence to pursue high-trust relationships.

Be clear about your ambitions. Why are you choosing trust? What are your expectations if you build more trusted relationships with colleagues, clients or suppliers? What are the benefits for you? Be as specific as possible and set yourself a measurable goal over time for measurable change.

Create a narrative about your value of trust based on your answer above, and make sure you are ready to share it. Your willingness to share it extends trust to others and gives them the opportunity to step up with their own extension of trust.

Match your behaviours to your narrative. How will you behave in meetings, on the phone, and by email? Are you able to demonstrate an alignment with your value of trust?

Commit and review. It takes positive effort of time and personal courage to try to transform or create relationships of trust. Make a commitment to yourself not only to make that investment, but also to set a timescale to review the plan you have created.

The point of emphasis here is that only by treating trust as a proactive investment are you likely to realise the potential that trust-based relationships can create.

The organisation trust mindset

Whatever your individual qualities, one of the biggest challenges many face is the context within which they operate. Whatever your personal intentions, how can you build trust if pressures from the organisation are in the opposite direction?

This is a question of culture. If strategy sets out what you plan to do, then culture is about how you will do it. This is the sum of behaviours practised by the organisation and should be captured by declared values. Yet in too many cases these are simply words on a wall, in head office or on a website.

Does your organisation have a value that is along the lines of: "We will work as one team", or "We will work together", or "We believe in collaboration"? How is this actively turned into real-world behaviours? This can be described as "turning values into value", and our experience suggests it is not often done. When it is done, it is typically inconsistent across the organisation or time.

Can you imagine values like the following?

- "We aim to maximise short-term profit from all of our customers."
- "We will screw rivals at every opportunity we get."
- "We will work our juniors into the ground."

No, but if that's what people actually do, then trust is damaged as the values are not backed up by behaviours. The same applies to meaningless phrases used as a strapline or value. If you can't define what this means in practice, then it chips away at trust because the organisation doesn't mean what it says. Hollow promises damage credibility – and that erodes trust.

The following exercise can help you demonstrate how

easy it is to create confusion in the language that people use. It highlights how often common language isn't the same as common understanding and how trust can easily break down.

Exercise: No guessing

1. Gather together your team or colleagues. Ask them to get into groups of two or three.

2. Give them a word and, in 60 seconds, ask them to write a list of all the meanings, metaphors and synonyms that come to mind.

   Choose a word that you and your colleagues use regularly in your business. A good example is the word "transaction".

3. When the time is up, ask each person to predict what percentage of words they might have in common with a colleague's list. Typical predictions will be anywhere from 25% to 75% words in common.

4. Now ask each person to compare their list with one or two others – the rule being they must have exactly the same word (on all lists) to score.

After a few seconds, get the scores from each group.

Most groups will have between zero and two exact matches. They will come nowhere near the 25%–75% predictions, and this will demonstrate that, even when people say the same words, they often mean something entirely different from each other.

It's the effort that goes into ensuring clarity of language *and definition* that creates trust, and it's the assumption that everyone will know what you mean that leads to misunderstanding, misdirected effort and frustration. The point here is that when team members all use the nominated word, they believe that everyone else means it in exactly the same way. This exercise shows that they don't. How much else is being done or said with the assumption that everyone knows what is meant – but isn't true?

A well-known business quote attributed to management guru Peter Drucker is: "Culture eats strategy for breakfast." In other words, what we actually do is more important than any ideas about what we should do.

On the issue of trust, this breaks down into two areas.

1. Do you choose to trust each other?
2. Do you choose trust as a competitive edge?

Do you trust each other?

In many organisations, internal relationships are highly transactional.

A client engaged us on a Europe-wide change project that promised to transform their customer experience. Yet the interaction between the European and country leadership and the in-house technology team was like the very worst type of client–supplier relationships. It had blame, disappointment and failure built into the process.

Those involved were challenged with this question: are you customers or colleagues? In both cases, the best way forward would be to behave collaboratively, solving problems together. With colleagues it should be clear from the start that everyone is on the same side. In this case, however, it wasn't.

As they explored this issue, it became clear that they had achieved the worst of all possible worlds: assuming colleague status (which removed the accountability for delivery) but behaving as if it was a client–supplier relationship (that is, highly transactional), which led to blame and conflict. Our work with them led to a reset of the relationship and the company is now driving the multi-year change programme with a completely different collective mindset.

What's important here is to build a team mindset and

continually reinforce and promote it. This should come from the top. Organisations should be designed to collaborate, not to compete. This is just as true at the team level, where too often the individual and their contribution are celebrated more than the success of joint effort and teamwork.

The structure of many organisations is still a reflection of Industrial Age thinking. Hierarchical, divisional, product, geographic organisations are defined around specialisation – easy to measure and control but also creating silos, competition for scarce resources and ultimately distrust. Separate departments like human resources, learning & development, risk management, internal audit, marketing, sales, business development are developed to value expertise and its application to tasks. Each department typically sets its own goals and strategies, and resource plans are created with scant regard to how they affect, support, benefit or even restrict others in meeting their goals.

Compare this with organisations whose leaders choose trust and are built to collaborate. The advantages are obvious. For example, as the world's largest social media platform, Facebook has played a significant role in connecting people and sharing information. However, this vast platform has also been exploited by terrorist organisations for recruitment, propaganda and coordination of attacks. In response to this challenge, Facebook established in 2016 what it called a tiger team to address the issue of terrorism on its platform.

The tiger team consisted of experts from across the business with knowledge of counter-terrorism, data analysis and social media, with input from other experts from the law enforcement community as well as educators with specific knowledge of counterterrorism. Meeting fortnightly, its mission was to identify, remove and prevent terrorist content from appearing on Facebook. The team employed a variety of strategies to achieve this goal, including:

- content moderation using increasingly sophisticated algorithms
- human review
- collaboration with law enforcement to gain and share the latest insight.

The tiger team has had a significant impact on the fight against terrorism on Facebook. According to Facebook's own data, the team has removed over 1.5 million pieces of terrorist content from the platform since its inception. Additionally, the team has helped law enforcement agencies to identify and arrest numerous terrorists.

This is a model of how tiger teams can be a valuable tool for addressing complex and evolving challenges. By bringing together experts from different fields and providing them with the resources they need, tiger teams can develop innovative solutions to problems that would be difficult to address using traditional methods.

This concept is now the basis for other successful collaborative organisations. By bringing together teams that focus on outcomes rather than protecting silos, these organisations harness cross-functional input for the most critical strategies and goals. This approach excites and engages employees to give their best efforts to the business, and may also reach out to engage their best suppliers, and even customers, who can contribute to mutually beneficial outcomes.

These organisations don't see their world through the lens of command and control: their constituent parts learn to trust each other. They know that mistakes will be made but the focus is on learning, fixing and moving forward rather than blame and shame. Trusting each other in this way, they achieve far greater results for themselves and their organisation. Tiger team organisations such as ARM, Ali Baba, Amazon and eBay form powerful ecosystems where they share goals and together create value far greater than any individual organisation could achieve.

In his book *The Seven Day Weekend*, Ricardo Semler describes his response to a serious business downturn in his country, Brazil, which was the opposite of what might have been expected.[6] As the owner of the family business Semco, he might have done what his rivals were doing – taking executive action to reduce costs, laying off workers and cutting wages. Instead, Semler chose trust.

Carefully explaining the situation to his staff, and laying out the challenges he saw, he created clarity and a commitment to solving the problems together. He then extended trust further by giving his employees the right to make any decision they felt was in their joint best interests – even down to how long they worked (hence the title of the book), how much they were paid and even how much *he* was paid. By treating them as colleagues and peers, who also of course wanted the business to survive and thrive, he turned conventional thinking completely on its head.

His action – extending trust – was met with reciprocity from the team, who subsequently shepherded the business to unrivalled success in its market, turning it from loss making to becoming the fastest growing business in South America.

Do you choose trust as a competitive edge?

In a transaction, the exchange of value is simple. Money is paid for a product or service or for the provision of labour. One side provides it, the other pays for it. If the product, service or work is deemed to be sub-standard, there is a dispute.

A trusted relationship feels completely different. There is recognition that the two sides are interdependent. They both want the best outcome and realise they both have responsibility for it. Money and a product or service are still involved, but there is much more going on. If you look at people involved in a trusted relationship, the way they interact is dynamic and collaborative, demonstrating a shared ambition and a sense of collective success or failure.

Even if the relationship is commercial, the two sides feel like a team. Is this how you would like to be with your customers? Or with your suppliers or partners?

In a trusted relationship, those involved enjoy their work more and therefore perform better.

- Mistakes or problems are tackled earlier (and together) because people share vulnerabilities and are open about challenges.

- Far greater value is created for everyone involved because they collaborate to find the best solutions together, with clarity about what both sides seek to gain from the relationship. This leads to new ideas and innovation.

- Because the relationship is strong, neither party seeks short-term gain at the expense of the other as there is an understanding that both sides rely on goodwill and future collaboration.

- The behaviours shown on a daily basis include honesty, openness, courage, celebration and mutual support.

The net result is that the customer gets the best service and outcome, price is much less of an issue, and there is loyalty and longevity in the relationship. Those involved stay longer at their organisations and get a stronger sense of satisfaction from their work. The supplier makes more money, the customer gets more value.

Here's an important question. If you had this relationship with your customers, would this give you a competitive edge?

Ah yes, people often say, but it takes two to tango. The customer has to want to engage in this kind of relationship. But think about that quote by Lao Tzu at the start of this chapter: "He who does not trust enough will not be trusted."

In other words, it starts with you. To be trusted, you have to be trustworthy and trusting. To achieve any trust-based relationship, you need consciously to want it and organisations deliberately have to put this ambition at the centre of its approach to customers. This is the organisation trust mindset in practice. It starts with the belief that this is how you choose to engage with customers, and both as an individual and as a business you are ready to say so.

The power of reciprocity will often kick in. But even if the customer does not change, evidence suggests they will still choose a more trusting and trustworthy organisation. And, ultimately, what type of organisation do you want to be?

The power of the trust mindset is that it establishes your organisation or team as the one that others will also choose. Setting out clearly what this means and how it works in practice creates an approach that really differentiates an organisation. As long as it is backed up by real behaviours, it becomes part of the narrative.

This takes us back to our starting point: to choose trust as the fundamental driver of sustainable value, and then to do something about it, behave accordingly and proactively design relationships that are based on high levels of trust.

What does this look like in practice? That's the focus of the next section of the book.

PART 2

The formula for trust

So, trust is critical. It's important to be intentional about it. What really makes a difference is to have a consistent method to establish and grow high-trust relationships. That is what this part of the book addresses.

In the introduction to the book, we defined trust. It has three dimensions, and these three Cs form the trust triangle: clarity, character and capability. By understanding each dimension, and using that knowledge to actively design trust, you have the power to make a difference in every working relationship you have.

Chapter 3 shows why clarity is the foundation of trust. It explores how often there is confusion, which causes distrust, and how to be clear with each other proactively in a way that sets a high ambition.

The way people behave in any relationship will affect trust and Chapter 4 looks at this in detail. The character of the relationship will be determined by the way those involved interact. It includes the five principles of behaviour – the most common behaviours that create trust.

There's a danger that you think about these issues and end up with warm words and empty promises. This is so often true in working relationships. That is why the relationship should be managed and governed in a way that makes sure the words are made true, and the value of working together is fully realised. This is what Chapter 5 addresses, dealing with the capability of the people involved to mean what they say and make sure they consistently build trust.

Every chapter has exercises you can use to put the theory into practice. However, the key is to focus on the big ideas and use these as an approach, an intention in the way you deal with other people. If you do that, with or without all the tools in this book, you won't go far wrong.

3

Clarity: the foundation of trust

"The beginning of wisdom is the definition of terms."

Socrates, Ancient Greek philosopher

A man says to his lawyer: "I want to divorce my wife."

"What are your grounds?"

"Grounds? We have quarter of an acre, mostly just lawn."

"No, that's not what I meant. Do you have a grudge?"

"No, just a carport."

"Well, does she beat you up?"

"No, I'm up by 6.30 and sometimes she doesn't get up until after I've left for work."

"Just tell me why you want a divorce!"

"My wife says we don't communicate."

This joke, an all-time favourite, highlights a simple reality. Two people may say the same thing as each other but each mean something completely different.

This statement is hugely profound. It is also the source of most mistrust, and so its opposite – being sure that both parties mean the same thing – can be the greatest source of trust. This, at its heart, is the trust dimension of *clarity*.

The actual problem is what happens next. You assume you both mean the same thing when you say, for example, "transformation" or "innovation". Or any one of many words and phrases that are used all the time in business with no clear and agreed definition. The people or teams involved then act according to their own understanding of what has been agreed and are shocked to discover that the other party – doing the same – is going in a different direction.

As was pointed out in a survey report from The Economist Intelligence Unit:

> Poor communication is having a tremendous impact on the workplace. ... Respondents say communication barriers are leading to a delay or failure to complete projects (44%), low morale (31%), missed performance goals (25%) and even lost sales (18%) – some worth hundreds of thousands of dollars.[1]

As a result, trust is damaged. When this happens, both parties end up dissatisfied with the experience even though they started out with the best intentions. The person commissioning the work says: "Next time, I'll watch every step to make sure they're doing what I expected." The person doing the work says: "Next time, I'll check in at every stage to make sure they'll pay me for the work I'm doing."

Innovation is no longer possible. Change is painful. The quality of the work will be less than it could have been. On major projects, everything slows down because of the constant need to check in. Disputes arise, blame begins and everyone becomes defensive about their behaviour.

That's why clarity is the foundation of the trust triangle. Clarity is much more than a formal contract, which still leaves ambiguities and fails to address change. People shake hands, intending to trust each other and be trustworthy, only for each to find that the other person has not done what they expected. The handshake turns to finger pointing, blame replaces agreement and trust is absent.

If you are to choose trust, you need to actively tackle the issue of clarity. As a start, it can help to recognise what often goes wrong.

Confusion as a source of mistrust

When the US Space Agency NASA launched the Mars Climate Orbiter (MCO) in 1998, it was an exciting project designed to study the climate, atmosphere and surface of our closest neighbour planet. It was the first mission of a wider programme designed to understand more fully what it is like on Mars, a precursor to further probes and – who knows – maybe eventual colonisation of the Red Planet.

Complex and pioneering technology was on board this mini-spacecraft, which was just over 2 metres tall. Highly sophisticated solar-powered engines and thrusters enabled the MCO to skim Mars's upper atmosphere, gradually slowing down through what is known as aerobraking. To do this, it had to be within a specific range of altitudes, and calculations suggested that the minimum that this needed to be for it to survive was 110 km (68 miles).

After nearly ten months on its journey to Mars, the mini-spacecraft headed into this procedure. Unfortunately, disaster struck. Its trajectory took it too close to the planet – a subsequent report showed that it was within 57 km (35 miles) of the surface. It skipped off the surface of the atmosphere and headed off into space. The mission was a failure.

What had gone wrong? Despite being a $327m programme, with top teams in both NASA and the builder of the mini-spacecraft, Lockheed Martin, there was one detail that they had overlooked: the two organisations were using different units of calculation to work out the force produced by the firing of the thrusters which directed the spacecraft. Whereas NASA had changed its procedures to use metric units, Lockheed Martin was still using traditional English measure of pounds. Fatally, an *assumption* was made by NASA that the data it was seeing was in the units it expected.

The official report on the incident stated:

> When conflicts in the data were uncovered, the team relied on email to solve problems, instead of formal problem resolution processes such as the Incident, Surprise, Anomaly (ISA) reporting procedure. Failing to adequately employ the problem tracking system contributed to this problem "slipping through the cracks".[2]

Slipping through the cracks! Instead of speaking to each other to sort things out, they sent an email and assumed the problem would be solved, somewhere. The difference in the calculations meant that over the ten-month mission, small errors occurred every time they worked out the trajectory of the spacecraft. By the time it reached Mars it was pointing in the wrong direction, and it was too late. The mini-spacecraft crashed and was destroyed.

There's a message here for many business relationships. Trust can be destroyed by what may initially be only a minor difference in belief about what you each mean. This divergence may start small, but it will grow during the life of the project or relationship, so that by the time it is critical it may be too late.

When people work together, they rarely set out to deliberately confuse others. But if you don't invest time in building a common understanding, confusion often occurs.

A number of factors concerning lack of clarity contribute

to the journey from a warm initial relationship to distrust and conflict.

Different meaning

The quote from Socrates at the start of this chapter sums it up: "The beginning of wisdom is the definition of terms."

The NASA story shows what happens when two people or organisations assume they mean the same thing. Here is an exercise you can do which can have a powerful impact. It's a variation on the "no guessing" exercise in Chapter 2.

Exercise: Different perceptions of reality

When you have the chance, sit down with the person you need to work with – a colleague, a supplier, a customer – and identify a critical word or phrase you will use frequently together. For example, you may be involved in a transformation, a change, or perhaps an implementation project. Pick one of these words which is meant to describe your mission together.

You should then both write down a list of definitions, associations or synonyms that sum up what you mean by this word or phrase. Give yourself up to 5 minutes.

Then compare the lists. Instead of simply identifying the differences (or similarities) in what you have written, use this as a basis for discussion. Going into detail about what each you understand by this word or phrase will demonstrate how even minor differences of perception can lead to major divergence of actions and behaviours.

For example, if, in a medical setting, you discuss the word "patient" and you have wildly different words associated with it, consider how this affects the way you respond to patients and treat them. The words that crop up may range from simply associating them with the condition you are treating to associating them with the person being treated. You might see a patient as a customer you serve, or as a person who benefits from your service. These are both true but are fundamentally different ways to perceive a patient.

This is an opportunity to align on some big issues with someone you need to trust and need to be trusted by, and to make sure when you say these key words you both mean the same thing.

Self-interest

This is about the lens through which people look when they work with others. Many start from the position that they are willing to commit to what needs to be done – but only in a way that links to *their* goals, *their* recognition and *their* rewards. Their self-interest overrides the potential benefits of teamwork.

There is a choice to be made here. If people decide not to explore the possibilities of collaboration and trust-based relationships early on, the result will be a discussion that at best focuses on compromise. By default, each party will use the lens of self-interest rather than focus on the benefit of the whole relationship. The result can be a confused mess – maybe an agreement that satisfies no one and is open to interpretation, or a working relationship that is characterised by blame and poor outcomes.

Misaligned systems and behaviours

Even within a single organisation, it's clear that internal systems – goal setting, measurement, recognition and reward – often create confusion between teams and reduce their ability to collaborate.

A sales team rewarded for achieving quarterly numbers potentially makes a poor partner for a delivery team paid for achieving annual margin or client satisfaction goals. A company that says it wants to build relationships over time drives its people to close deals to hit short-term targets. A CEO explains that she wants to empower her team, but then issues commands she expects to be carried out, whether or not the people involved agree. This is the classic recipe for a lack of clarity: conflicting signals that drive different people to varied behaviours that result in poorer outcomes.

Confirmation bias

Confirmation bias is the ability of the brain to hear or see things that support existing beliefs and ignore those that do not. Anyone who has long experience of failure in "collaborative" relationships will have a predisposition not to trust. It's little wonder that their experience then guides their behaviours. Confirmation bias sets the expectations of those involved and each party feeds the bias of the others if they behave in a self-oriented way. Our brain finds the data that supports our beliefs.

This has been what many experience as the normal way of doing business. And, of course, many have had success in doing so, which reinforces the confirmation bias. However, that leaves little room to consider what might have been possible with a different approach.

If you are to choose trust as a potential source of much greater value, you need to break out of this particular cycle of belief.

Clarity as a source of trust

Think back to the story of John Neill and Unipart in Chapter 2. This was the story of a major deal reached with a huge potential client, Jaguar, based on a clear, shared vision. Huge value was created by aligning the interests of both parties, founded on a mutual understanding of their collective ambition.

It's no surprise to discover that a leader like Neill applies the same principles to his employees. His behaviours reflect a core belief that organisations and people who want to be trusted need to demonstrate trustworthiness in all directions, both internally and externally. High-trust leadership underpins high-trust business development.

Neill had learned the Japanese principles of "lean production" from engineers at Honda and Toyota – an approach that is based on an obsession to remove waste and, critically, to involve employees at every stage in the process. He then applied these principles successfully in the UK, and embedded them into a manifesto of how he wanted the company to be led. He called it the Unipart Way. It was a radical document when it was written in 1987. It remains a beacon of how to develop a clear and consistent vision, not because it contains words that became widely used by others, but because it has genuinely driven the behaviours, culture and strategy of the company in demonstrable ways since then.

Here, in summary, is what drove John Neill in his own words.

> We had to create a new business model, and you have to try to communicate these things in an authentic way ... that's graspable and re-tellable by everybody in the company.[3]

This is clarity in action: a set of principles that everyone involved can understand. How Neill did this was to characterise the past as Model A, which was about adversarial, short-term power-based relationships with the stakeholders: for example, pricing that maximised the transactional value with the customer for today with no concern for tomorrow or battling suppliers to get the cheapest price even if it destroyed their business.

Neill promised instead to implement what he called New Model B. This had the stated aim of creating customers for life, with what he described as "shared destiny relationships with stakeholders". This involved training staff to deliver high-quality customer service, and the "strategic intent to keep people working with Unipart forever".

A similar long-term view was taken with suppliers and the local community. Neill's belief was: "If we do all of those things, we'll produce fair, enduring, long term returns for our shareholders."

Today, as well as manufacturing and logistics, Unipart consults with other firms on how to apply the Unipart Way principles. Its customers are long term and work with the firm in a high-trust way that builds mutual value, always starting with a joint vision of what they are trying to achieve. Every employee, customer and other stakeholder is given a copy of the Unipart Way brochure that sets out the principles by which the firm is run.

Clarity is the ability to define a shared intent and outcome – a clear ambition – that enables people to behave consistently with that intent, and to agree measures and rewards for achieving a desired outcome. This ambition needs to be easily understood and communicable to everyone involved. In a large organisation, that requires simplicity and focus.

When we say that clarity is the foundation of the trust triangle, we mean that when you choose trust, you need to achieve clarity before anything else. And that is where the problem often lies. Typically, people want to get straight into action, to go from commitment to delivery. The focus is on *doing* not *understanding*. This is so often the reason that mistrust results, because those involved go off in different directions. Instead, consider why a high-trust approach will work. It requires an investment of time right at the start to ensure mutual understanding, but this will pay back many times over in the results that will be achieved.

Let's start with why. What happens when you choose trust and achieve clarity?

Shared passion and commitment: the "why"

By building clarity of ambition – by being clear about what they want to achieve together – people start to build shared emotional commitment to the outcome. Voicing the purpose and benefits of the relationship or the partnership is an important part of the trust-building process. This creates a powerful "why".

Focusing first on the "why" and not the "how" is a powerful way to identify and capture the passion and commitment of those involved and gain real insight into what matters to everyone involved.

One direction

This is where a clear vision is so important. Alignment is critical to create the best outcome when people or organisations work together. The Unipart and Mars Climate Orbiter stories demonstrate that. Two aeroplanes that take off one degree apart and stay on those headings will end up in different countries.

Even minor misalignment results in people arriving in different places – and wondering why the other person isn't there.

Mutual understanding

At this stage, it's important to define terms clearly. For example, the word "partnership"; what does it mean in practice? And what does it look like when things go wrong? This is about proactively ensuring that the Mars Climate Orbiter experience does not happen. Make sure everyone involved has a shared understanding of what you aim to do and how.

If you are confident that you understand and are understood by the other party, trust is more likely to be present.

Pre-emptive issue resolution

Investing time early on allows issues to be raised and resolved in the planning stage. If you know how you will resolve issues and disputes, and you follow through in a consistent way, you reduce the chance that any challenges – which will inevitably occur – will destroy trust.

This is a perfect time to tackle these issues. When the parties are hungry to get on with the work, and know what they want to achieve together, there will be more goodwill around, so this is the time to talk about what can go wrong and how you will work together to solve it. This involves discussion of agreed behaviours and the governance of the relationship – issues that will be explored in Chapters 4 and 5.

These principles apply both at the start of major relationships – such as a big project – and in a daily context. For example, at the start of meetings, be clear together about why you have met, what your ambition is for that discussion and check in to make sure this is true throughout the session. When you begin even a small piece of work with others, apply the same thinking: get clarity on why you are doing this, how you will do it and what you want to achieve together.

This idea can be a practical approach to even the most straightforward transactions. For example, when you get someone into your house to repair something, be sure you are both clear on why you want the work done, your hope and ambition for the benefits, and agreement that this is what the person will do for the agreed cost. This kind of discussion will give them scope to suggest a better way to tackle the issue: your "why" is what counts; their "how" is what they bring.

Gaining clarity may even result in a better outcome than you had expected.

How to be clear

In 2014 two giants of the technology world, Apple and IBM, announced a partnership with a very specific ambition: to transform how businesses operate by combining the power of mobile technology and enterprise software. This is the software – the applications and the way they work together – used by large organisations to run their businesses.

The ambition for this partnership was also clear. Apple and IBM aimed to create business-specific mobile applications that would enhance productivity, streamline processes and improve decision-making for their customers.

Sounds great. But this partnership had history. The two companies started as fierce rivals when they both produced personal computers in the 1980s. In 1981, Apple even produced a cheeky ad which welcomed IBM to the personal computer market that Apple claimed it had invented.

But in 1991, Apple engineers approached IBM to show how its software could work on an IBM computer. They saw IBM as the gateway to the business market, and the Taligent project was born. For a time, this looked like challenging Microsoft's dominance in software, but by 1998 the alliance had run out of steam and Taligent was absorbed back into IBM. Changes in personnel appear to have been at the heart of the collapse, with the original visionaries no longer there.

So why would a partnership succeed this time? The clarity of vision to combine the strengths of both firms was critical. IBM had world-leading expertise in data, artificial intelligence, enterprise software, the challenges of its huge base of business customers and deep sales presence in the space. Apple brought its unique knowledge of mobile-first applications, user experience, machine learning and, of course, proprietary ownership of iOS (the Apple operating system for its mobile devices), which puts it in an unparalleled position in the marketplace.

Within 18 months *CIO World* was celebrating the news that the Apple/IBM team had released 100 apps that targeted 65 professions across 14 industries.[4] Active collaboration has led to IBM being able to promise its customers the ability to combine the best of these two giant corporations, connecting leading-edge technologies with the huge IBM infrastructure geared towards the biggest customers.

The big "why" drove collaboration and ensured the teams worked out how to succeed together.

How can you create a similar vision for the high-trust relationship you choose to build? There are three key questions you need to answer, ideally with the other person or party.

Who will benefit from this relationship?

The core task when building trust with clarity is to identify *why* you want to come together to create value. The first question to ask concerns the people or organisations who will gain value from the collaboration. What better outcome can you achieve together? Framing the relationship in these terms means the relationship will be more successful because it is focused on outcomes, not processes.

This involves discussion about the following.

· Who exactly are the people who will benefit? This should be explored in as precise terms as possible. This analysis will include those involved in the delivery as well as those who are the end users of the work being done together. As a team ask: what outcomes do we need to achieve for ourselves? And what outcomes do we need to achieve for those we serve? Depending on the scale of the undertaking, the range of people involved may be broad or narrow.

- Organisations the size of IBM and Apple can identify any large businesses as their target. IBM and Apple were clear that these types of organisations had new needs to use software on the move and that there were describable benefits of doing so.

- Smaller organisations need to be more precise. For example, at the other end of the scale, a coffee shop establishing a relationship with a bookshop might define its target group as "people in the town of Littleton who visit the high street and have time to have a coffee", together with the owners of the two businesses who want to increase their revenues through cross-selling.

- Similarly, teams developing high-trust relationships should frame their collaboration in terms of the customers that their organisation serves or, if they are providing internal focused services, the people who use their services. For example, a technology team developing a better working relationship with a project delivery team might frame the outcome in terms of the benefits to the customer-facing parts of the business. But they will also look inwards and put themselves into the equation: how will both teams benefit from developing a deeper, trusting relationship?

- As for those who will benefit, what do they care about? In other words, what is their "why"?

This last question is designed to focus your mind on the value you want to create in terms of what matters to the people who are meant to benefit. As an example, if one party is a highways department and the other is a prime contractor building a road, the outcome will be in terms of the end benefit to road users (time saved, easier journey, access to a specific town or city), the economy (estimated financial benefit), and any other factors (this might include lower pollution through shorter journeys, use of technology to ease congestion, more charging points for electric vehicles on the new route).

For the bookshop and coffee shop, the benefits might be to provide a great place to read, financial savings through cross-promotion, and a sense of community in the high street.

IBM and Apple were very clear. The large businesses they were targeting had increasingly mobile workforces who needed to be able to do their work on the move. In the case of every piece of software, there were easily described benefits for making it easy for them to do so.

The narrative of this relationship was grounded in the "whys" of their customers, and so those involved were all focused in that direction.

Where can you co-create value?

Consider what can you do together that you cannot do separately. What value does this create for the people you serve? A good way to begin is with the simple model shown in Figure 4 on the next page.

Working this out can be the basis of a better relationship. And it demonstrates the intention to partner, not simply to transact.

If you are to work well with another person or other people, you will co-create value. You are interdependent. Building trust

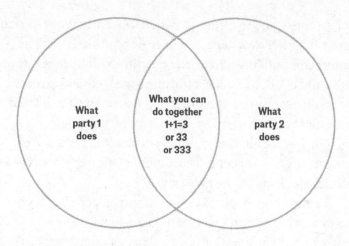

Figure 4: **The mutual ambition model**

enables you to make a relationship that is much more than simply combining your services or talents. The ambition should be to create more value than the sum of your parts. Can you make $1 + 1 = 3$? Or even better, 33? Or even 333? What does that look like?

This is thinking in terms of multiplication, not addition. IBM and Apple believed that, together, they had far greater potential than each of them had separately, even though they are among the world's largest corporations. They could have simply contracted one another for services, or indeed grown their own version of what the other offered. They decided instead to partner, to create mutual benefit and multiply the possibilities, enabling each to focus on areas where it was great. This is certainly true of you and your situation, whatever that may be.

Are you simply exchanging value, or instead building more value together? Even opening up this discussion can in itself be a powerful way to challenge existing norms and explore new possibilities of what you want to achieve and how ambitious you are.

If you are a buyer, you may think you have the power. But as soon as you have made the purchase, a lot of power shifts to the seller. The same applies to leaders with their teams. They are always interdependent. So it is much better to clarify right at the start the mutual ambition you have and make that the point of reference for everything you do.

How will you work together?

The way you work together will define how much trust is established and grown. If you are to choose trust, then it must be central to the establishment of any relationship.

Remember people's tendency to rush into action. When the focus is on delivery, it often comes at the cost of relationships. What ruins most interactions are the behaviours of those involved and the failure to identify how the relationship will be governed, managed and nurtured.

This will be explored more fully in Chapter 5 on capability. At this stage, what is important is to be clear (ideally with the others involved) about the nature of the relationship.

It could be that you want to be partners, or that you are a supplier and a customer who want to make a project successful – or that you are colleagues who want to collaborate more fully. This last situation seems obvious, but experience suggests that people working for the same organisation do not always see themselves as being on the same team. It is a perfect situation for trust to be destroyed, but also one where going through this structured relationship design process will reap enormous benefits. Sometimes it is worth remembering that you are both serving the same purpose and so need to see the world in the same way.

Exercise: Being clear (1)

Consider a key relationship you have or want to develop. Look at each of the following questions in the context of this relationship and fill in your thinking. Keep it simple and top level; one or two ideas per question is ideal.

When you have done this, consider doing the same exercise with the other party or parties in the relationship. To what extent do the answers you develop together converge with those you developed alone?

Who benefits from our relationship?

Precise definition of who they are	*Answer*
What do they care about?	*Answer*

What value do the parties create together?

Areas where we excel	*Answer*
Areas where they excel	*Answer*
Our joint value proposition	*Answer*

How will the parties work together?

What is the nature of our relationship?	*Answer*

Your ambition

At the end of this process those involved should have a clear and agreed idea of who they serve, why, and how. This is a good moment to bring this together into an overall vision for the relationship – setting out a clear ambition of what they can achieve together.

This is different from the value proposition. It is a statement of purpose, underpinned by the answers to the questions above. Everything else is input into this vision, which creates a clear focus for the relationship as it currently stands and should seek to create a stretch ambition that is much bigger than simply collaborating to do the work.

Let's take an example. Suppose you run a human resources team and you're establishing a high-trust relationship with the communications team in your company. So many such relationships are highly transactional, with the teams doing their work in parallel. The aim here is to change that dynamic.

Exercise: Being clear (2)

Examples of top-level answers

Who benefits from our relationship?

Precise definition of who they are	*All our directly employed staff* *Potential staff members* *Leaders of our businesses who need us to be effective*
What do they care about?	*Staff: values and culture, doing their job well, developments in the business, how it affects them, chances of developing their career, pay and conditions* *Potential staff members: potential of the business, plus all the above* *Leaders: engaged staff, team mentality, high performance, values and culture, personal ambitions*

What value do the parties create together?

Areas where we excel	*People as part of company strategy, culture and values, people development*
Areas where they excel	*Engagement, outreach to potential staff, reputation, storytelling*
Our joint value proposition	*High performing, highly engaged people, who know what's happening, care and love working here*

How will the parties work together?

What is the nature of our relationship?	*We are collaborative colleagues working alongside each other, serving the wider business*

Going into some more detail beneath these top-level entries will help the discussion – for example, a breakdown of the types of staff will help colour the discussion about how the teams work together. A company with frontline staff out in the field, for example, would benefit from a discussion about how best to engage those people and embed them in the company culture. Here's where 1 + 1 = 33. What might have been separate communications to these staff can now be combined; for example, training and internal communications can be synchronised and the people involved receive just one information feed.

Working together, this team can set out a powerful ambition which is set within the broader strategy of the firm. It may result in a statement like this.

> We want our people to love working here and be motivated to outperform our competitors. That's why we will consistently grow the level of expertise and engagement among our people, ensuring they know what's happening, care and are able to actively contribute to a dynamic culture. We will track this to ensure it happens and connects directly to the performance of the business.
>
> We will celebrate this through powerful storytelling, and use these stories to build the reputation of the firm externally to attract high-quality people.
>
> The HR and marketing teams will work together in line with our company values, in a spirit of openness and honesty as great colleagues, collaborating to achieve this collective ambition. Our teams' relationship will be reviewed every quarter to make sure we are being consistent with this commitment.

Exercise: What is your ambition?

Consider a key relationship you or your team has. If you have filled in the grid above, use it to consider what a great ambition would be for that relationship. If you have not yet competed the grid, do that first; alternatively, do the following as a thought experiment.

What would be a fantastic vision for this relationship, which would create the most value for everyone involved? How might you articulate that?

Write it down.

And how powerful would it be to have such a vision agreed with the others involved in the relationship, consistently reviewed to make sure you're focused on achieving it?

If you have completed the exercises in this chapter, it will be clear that thoughtfully investing time and effort to build shared clarity with those with whom you wish to build strong relationships is an investment worth making.

However, this will only have a lasting impact if you make this statement true through your behaviours and the way you manage the relationship. That is what the next two chapters will address, starting with the behaviours of a high-trust relationship: its character.

4

Character: the behaviours that build trust

"Trust is built with consistency."

Herodotus, Ancient Greek historian

In the Arnold Schwarzenegger *Terminator* films, an artificial intelligence (AI) defence system, Skynet, becomes self-aware. Thus starts the rise of the machine and the attempted destruction of the human race.

In the first film, Schwarzenegger is a cyborg assassin who returns from what was once the distant future to 1984, where his mission is to kill the mother of a man who will one day lead the fight against Skynet. That distant future was 2029. It is no longer a remote year that is almost unimaginable. And the Terminator is often used as a shorthand to express the fears about AI which is right here, right now.

What's already true is that AI is starting to take on tasks that were once purely the preserve of humans, from creating art, photography and poetry, to helpdesk responses, as well as automating much of the repetitive work that has to date underpinned many jobs and professions.

The fear is that, as a result, millions of jobs are at risk. AI can impersonate humans – even their voices and images – and already does many of the things that people can do. So where does that leave people, organisations and companies who want to succeed in the market?

The answer is based in our humanity. Real humans will, for the foreseeable future, always be better than the artificial version in at least one area: connecting at an emotional level with another person and forming trusted relationships. Increasingly, simply being a high-performing unit of labour will not help you beat the machine, as there is a good chance it will overtake you.

Your best shot is to be more human, to build trust – and central to this are your behaviours. The ideal outcome is that there are high-trust behaviours from everyone involved so that they characterise your relationship. That is why character is one of the three dimensions of trust, and this chapter looks deeply at the behaviours that flow from your character and how people perceive them.

The way that people work together – *how* they do what they do – often determines the success of the relationship at least as much as *what* they are doing and how well they can do it.

Whatever your work context, people study your behaviour to assess whether it's aligned with what you have said. They may not do it consciously, but that is what happens. What they experience helps them decide if your behaviour is consistent and therefore predictable and trustworthy.

Predictability is perhaps the most critical element of trusted relationships. How much do you trust somebody whose reaction you can't predict in any situation? Think about a boss who one day meets a problem with calm resolution and the next day blows up like a tornado. This unpredictability makes the boss untrustworthy and team members become wary of raising issues with them. Worse still, they may fear appearing untrustworthy themselves.

The difference made by high-trust behaviours

Consistent, aligned behaviours – the "how" – are crucial when you choose trust. Let's consider what difference it makes when you develop high-trust behaviours.

Trustworthiness

Measures of trust in business such as the Edelman Trust Barometer Global Report tell us that levels of trust in advanced economies have been broadly falling in recent years.[1] Perhaps not surprisingly, our predilection to trust is reducing as well. Polarisation between and within countries is increasing, and trust in government and media is heading to an all-time low.

Trust seems to be in short supply and mistrust is on the rise everywhere. But although it makes no sense to trust everything and everyone, it is no better to wait for others to prove they are trustworthy. The starting point for being trustworthy is to extend trust. This is about going first – not waiting for the other person or business to prove worthy of your trust before demonstrating it yourself or seeing trust as something to repay transactionally.

You can choose trust by acting in an appropriate way and expect that most people will respond to your trustworthiness by being trustworthy in return. If they do not, that tells you something important and should inform your decision about whether to work with them.

Human beings like to be trusted and like to trust. By developing your capability to be trustworthy you can create relationships that become your competitive advantage in the market. It enhances your ability to adapt to change and continuously innovate, far outstripping your transactional competition.

Once trustworthiness has been established, the people involved in the relationship need to cultivate capability. You can do this by exhibiting some key qualities, such as:

- refusing to step back from trust into defensiveness, self-interest and distrust
- being open to being challenged by others and willing to question your own ideas
- checking that you continue to being open to sharing
- being open to listening carefully and understanding what others think and believe.

Let's consider this idea by using the belief model introduced in Chapter 1 (Figure 2, p. 33). This is the idea that our beliefs drive our actions, and that those actions create outcomes that tend to reinforce our beliefs.

When confronted with a question about a strongly held belief, the transactional thinker tends to hold to their view: being right is important to them. As a result, they quickly fall into defensive behaviour that often results either in the question falling away or at best in some kind of compromise.

This differs from the behaviour of somebody who values trust and has cultivated trustworthiness. These individuals meet challenge with an open mind. They approach the issue with the attitude that the person challenging them wants the best outcome for all, or may have different insights or different information. As such, their action is to listen and to build understanding.

Having listened and understood, those who lead with trust may be able to bring the challenger around to a shared understanding of their original thinking. Alternatively, they may learn something from the process that changes their own understanding and changes their action. Or the discussion may lead to a new insight or innovation for both parties.

In all these interactions, whatever the outcome, collaborative discussions where each party is willing to understand the other's point of view and is willing to learn, always strengthen the relationship between the parties. This is in contrast to challenge and defence, an approach that often leads to a sense of dissatisfaction for one or both.

Differentiation through consistency

One of us recently bought a property and needed a lawyer. The recommended firm successfully carried out the conveyancing, but it was difficult to speak directly to the lawyer involved. Instead, Stuart was constantly fobbed off by the people answering the phone, who gave him functional answers but kept telling him the lawyer was far too busy to speak to him.

Not only did Stuart hate dealing with the firm; he did not trust that everything was being done well. He had no idea whether the lawyer was taking things seriously, checking all the details which would make the difference between a successful and an unsuccessful transaction.

Then suddenly, towards the end of the process, he got a call early one morning. It was from the lawyer who was managing his case. She was a locum, filling in for the actual lawyer who was away on holiday. But she'd spotted something that needed to be addressed and wanted to talk it through. He was delighted to do so and as a result an important detail was tackled. He also had complete confidence that she was across everything. Just that one call was enough to build trust in her, but her behaviour contrasted so sharply with the way things had been managed previously that he decided not to use that firm again.

The difference lies not in *what* you do but *how* you do it. And that means an organisation as a whole as well any individuals. It's about relying less on the particular strengths of one person and more on a clearly thought-through approach to trust more generally. Personal interaction drives trust: people buy the experience they have as much as the functional outcome.

The foundation is consistency in behaviours in every touchpoint between an organisation and the people with whom it interacts: its customers or clients, its supply chain, its employees, its stakeholders and the wider public, whose opinion could influence its success in the future.

The quote from Herodotus, a fifth-century BC Greek historian, at the start of this chapter states: "Trust is built with consistency." It's this consistency of behaviours that creates the trust and trusted relationships that drive differentiation. People choose people and organisations that behave in consistently positive ways.

Bear in mind that rebuilding trust once you have lost it takes far more effort than maintaining it. A colleague compares trust in a relationship with a bank account. When he talks about how behaviours affect our "bank balance" in a trusted relationship, he simply says: "You deposit in pennies, but you withdraw in pounds." It's a powerful thought.

Exercise: Test your consistency

How consistent are you? Consider scenarios that may have happened at work and assess yourself on a scale of 0 to 10. A score of 0 would mean you are totally inconsistent; a score of 10 would mean you always respond in the same way, no matter who is involved or how important your response is to the other people involved.

Some examples are on the next page:

1. You made a mistake that means an important task can't be completed to time or to quality.

2. You are aware that the results for the business are disappointing because you are privy to confidential information. A worried employee asks you if the business issues might put their role under threat. How do you respond?

3. It's widely known that a more senior person makes inappropriate personal remarks about a colleague. They do it again in front of you. What do you do?

These situations may not be things you have experience with, so think of others and then ask yourself some questions. Do I behave consistently? Do I treat my employees or team members the same way I treat my boss or their boss?

The higher your scores and the more consistent you are across all categories, the more easily you will establish trusted relationships. People will not only observe your behaviour once, but the fact that they see it repeated time and time again tells them you can be trusted. They can then feel confident in knowing how you will react in any given situation.

When you're choosing trust, you need to be consistent with behaviours that build trust more quickly and deeply.

Better change

Change is a constant, whether that's in a major change programme or a rapidly evolving business environment. You might find this exciting or you might not, but almost every change project or initiative will hit some kind of unexpected obstacle or itself be subject to change. Ask any experienced project manager: "What's the one thing you know about this project?" and they will almost certainly reply: "It won't be exactly as we planned."

Think of the litany of large-scale government and construction projects that consistently fail to deliver on time, on budget and to specification. A prime example in the UK is

HS2 – a high-speed rail link between London and major cities in the north of England.[2] At the time of writing, the project is ten years late, hugely over the initial budget and is being reduced in ambition in the light of the cost overruns, no longer aiming to connect beyond the Midlands, and until 2040 terminating outside London.

The UK is not alone in failing to complete large projects on time and on budget. In 2007, the state of Texas initiated a project to implement a child support enforcement system. Massively late and over budget, the project was finally abandoned in 2020 with no tangible benefits. As Texas state representative Giovanni Capriglione, a local politician, commented: "This was a $60 million idea – $340 million ago."[3]

There seems to be something about these and many other projects that leads highly experienced procurement teams to figuratively square up to some of the most experienced potential suppliers. At the core of the problem is an overreliance on transactional thinking that replaces relationships, trust and personal contact with contract provisions. When change is needed, the people involved respond in ways that are untrusting and untrustworthy, because the relationship was always contractual. The results speak for themselves.

Instead, choosing trust brings massive benefits. In any project, things may go wrong. Or the world changes and there is a need to adapt quickly, often in ways that are outside the existing contract or agreement.

If there is real trust between the parties involved, none of this is life-threatening to the relationship. Many of us have had experiences where something has gone wrong or somebody has let us down, but what defines whether to continue to trust them is how they fix things. Do they acknowledge the error, do they take responsibility and hold themselves accountable? Do they actively try to right the wrong? These behaviours can turn a difficulty into a relationship builder, where trust in the other party is enhanced rather than damaged.

Prove this to yourself. Take a moment to think about a situation where you felt let down; perhaps a colleague or supplier did not perform as you expected.

- How did they respond when you raised the issue?
- Did they make excuses, or did they accept responsibility?
- Did they make good for the problem they created?
- Or, even better, did you resolve the issue together in a collaborative way?

Now reflect: do you trust them more or less? Would you recommend them to a friend or colleague?

Trusted partners sort things out together and behave in ways that maintain trust. When things go wrong in a transactional relationship, the parties tend to blame each other and reach for the contract. And that is where money gets lost, projects overrun, trust is lost and relationships are destroyed.

You get chosen

High-trust behaviours build more profitable, long-term and higher-value relationships. That means that you provide a better service, whatever you're doing and whoever you work with. The right consistent, trust-building behaviours will give you an advantage, which means the person you want to influence is more likely to choose you.

A good example is in the field of selling business services. Our research shows that business buyers choose suppliers for the following four reasons.

1. Technical capability: they can do the job.

2. Business case: the cost is reasonable for the work.

3. Cultural alignment: they share similar values.

4. Teamworking: they look like a team, not a set of different individuals.

Guess which are the top two factors? Yes, the last two: trust-building and cultural factors are more important than technical capability and price in winning business consistently. It's often the case that a supplier wouldn't be under consideration if they didn't tick the first two boxes. Yet almost all the work done in business development focuses on the other two factors.

The same applies in most situations. Where there's a choice as to who to promote, who to have as a supplier or partner, or which colleague to work with on a project, the person selected is likely to be the one who is most trusted.

Designing trust behaviours in your relationships

Choosing trust is a deliberate act. Trusted relationships need to be built with design so that there is consistency.

When this is done at an organisational level, you rely less on the particular strengths of one person and more on a broad trust of the whole team or organisation. This leads to what is a new approach to many: reaching out to those with whom you need a trusting relationship and investing time in that relationship to define the behaviours that will support it. These must be specific, visible and preferably measurable behaviours that all parties agree they will demonstrate, especially when faced with difficult times.

Instead of jumping straight in and "getting on with it" – doing the work the way you think is right – spend time focusing on the quality of the relationship. This makes it more likely that the work will be successful.

The five behaviours of trust

Our experience suggests that there are five common behaviours that people can adopt to build high-trust relationships.

TABLE 1. THE FIVE BEHAVIOURS OF TRUST

Consideration *Fairness*	· Actively seek value for all parties over and above short-term personal gain · The relationship is the focus, not the individuals · The value created for both parties is fair and equitable
Courage *Proactive trust*	· Put the vision and relationships first, actively seeking mutual value · Consciously ignore short-term gain for yourself · Act as a peer, not a subservient partner
Honesty *Openness*	· Be open, straightforward, and never duplicitous · Behave with high levels of integrity · Do not distort, spin or manipulate · Confront uncomfortable truths · Do not be corrupt in any way
Loyalty *Commitment*	· Give credit where credit is due · Live the Golden Rule: do unto others as you would have them do unto you, and believe that the integrity and intent of others matches your own · Talk about others as if they were present · Be aware of the needs of those who are absent and include them in your thinking · Demonstrate the belief that the relationship transcends any individual transaction
Ambition *Thinking bigger*	· Innovate · Harness the power of co-creation: 1 + 1 = 3 or 33 or 333 · Share resources and ideas to create better outcomes · Ambition as multiplication not addition: 1 x 2 x 3 x 4 · Constant and never-ending improvement

As you look at each of these principles in more detail, think about how you can apply them to your own relationships.

Consideration

When you choose trust, you commit yourself to being considerate to others as a basis for a successful relationship. But what does this really mean?

Being considerate is about making sure you understand what the other party in the discussion or relationship is trying to achieve. But here's the critical point. Consideration is not only about what an individual is talking about; it's also about building a deep understanding of what success looks like for them in the eyes of others who are important to them.

Relationships at work come in various forms but they all have one thing in common. Any relationship that endures will do so because it creates mutual value. Many will be able to describe such an outcome as win–win; very few understand what it takes to create consistent outcomes that are valuable to both sides. At the heart of this ambition is consideration.

The best place to start is by not guessing. Try to sit down with your opposite number and be curious. Ask them some fundamental questions about how things look from their perspective.

- What are you hoping to achieve?
- What would success for you look like?
- Who else is involved who has an interest in success?

Maybe you are trying to build relationships with external organisations – suppliers, customers or clients. This brings special risks as too often you assume that the person you are talking to knows or understands what everybody else in their organisation is trying to achieve in the context of your discussion. Or you worry that if you ask to talk to other people you might somehow upset the relationship.

What's important is that they understand that your intent is based on consideration for their success. Meeting others who affect the success of your opposite number, and deepening their understanding as well as yours, helps define a vision of success that will satisfy all stakeholders and helps create the conditions to achieve it.

Being considerate goes further than mere inquiry, however. It is ultimately about testing your opposite number's beliefs and vision for success. It may be that they do not fully understand the potential value that you can create together; they are looking at things from their level of experience, and you may have additional knowledge about what is possible.

As ever, your intent is critical. If you share this information to gain advantage, or simply to sell, this will show. If you do so with the principle of consideration at the heart of your actions, it will feel very different.

Exercise: Test your consideration

At any point in a relationship, you can ask yourself these questions to establish whether you have applied the behaviour of consideration in the way you have engaged with each other.

- Have I spent face-to-face time with my opposite number to explore how they define success?

- Am I confident from experience that this is the best that can be achieved – and that the parties believe they can achieve their desired outcomes?

- Have I shared my thinking or any challenge with my opposite number?

- Have I identified all the critical stakeholders affected by this discussion?

- Have I fully understood what success means to them?

Courage

If you have explored and tested your opposite number's vision for success, you can now demonstrate courage to explore your vision with them too. Your opportunity to do this well will be heavily influenced by the time and effort you put into consideration.

In this context, courage is the ability to stand up for your own interests and be clear that the value to be created is mutual, not one-sided. If your intent to create value for them is clear, they will be more open to understanding your position and working creatively towards meeting your needs as well as their own.

Beyond that, it's about ensuring that your courage extends to members of your team or company who may be involved in the delivery or continuing relationships. Being courageous on behalf of your colleagues means you build trust with them.

Compare this with the behaviour seen too often in transactionally minded people, for example in a sales environment. Under pressure to meet targets and faced with a client demanding a reduction in price, the transactional salesperson defaults to short-term thinking and gives in.

The results to the relationship in the longer term are clear. The client believes that whatever price they are being quoted by this salesperson is a lie and will be reduced on demand. The company will have to try to deliver goods or services at a lower margin than they need. This can result in that company trying to reduce the cost of delivery, which will affect the quality. Those involved with delivery often end up resenting both the client for putting them under such pressure and their colleague for giving in to the pressure in the first place. Trust and relationship are eroded on all sides.

The alternative requires the courage on behalf of the salesperson to be prepared to walk away from a bad deal and to keep integrity in the relationship. They need the confidence to explore the value they are trying to create with the client and to look at whether the deal they are suggesting is truly win-win. Being courageous is the opposite of subservience, and establishes a partnership geared towards delivering real value for everyone.

Exactly the same principle applies in whatever situation you address, because the people you're dealing with will see that you have clarity about your purpose and principles which you hold dear. This builds trust.

Exercise: Test your courage

Either on your own, or preferably with others in your team, review the following questions and make a note of the answers.

- Have you spent time with your own team to understand what success looks like and means to them?
- Have you made it clear to the other party in the relationship what you need as an outcome?
- Have you documented expectations and shared them both internally and externally?

Honesty

Honesty is about being straightforward, open and matching your words with actions. Many people, especially when under pressure, find it difficult to behave in a manner that reflects this kind of definition. But those who do earn the trust of everybody they meet.

Difficulties often arise when there is conflict between the goals that a transactional organisation creates and the knowledge that our behaviour may destroy trust in any relationship.

For example, a sales team invests time and money in bidding for a contract. They come to realise that the client has asked for something that could be done more effectively or doesn't need to be done at all. If they say nothing, they can win the transaction and meet their revenue and profit goals. Or they could be honest with the client and share their insight. What is your experience or expectation in this situation?

The norm is that the short-term transaction thinking takes priority and honesty goes out of the window.

Being honest, even when that means confronting unpalatable truths, even when it may mean taking a short-term hit to revenue, cost or profit, is always the winning behaviour for trusted relationships. Choosing trust means thinking beyond the transaction and perhaps beyond the specific opportunity you face today. People and organisations that choose trust behave in a way that builds personal, team and organisational credibility, which can have far-reaching impacts on their success.

A key component to honesty is openness. This includes the idea of being transparent, so that nothing is hidden and the people you are dealing with know they can see everything they need to and so judge your character.

Loyalty

If you want to have successful relationships, it's critical to demonstrate loyalty on two levels.

1. Loyalty to the relationship: understanding and demonstrating a commitment to a shared ambition, and

the concept of mutual value, achieving a goal that is meaningful and valuable to both parties, not just one of them.

2. Loyalty to the people in the relationship, whether in your own organisation or externally.

Changing your mindset to adopt a relationship approach based on trust asks that you resist the gravity of beliefs based on cynicism and short-term self-interest. If you are to do this successfully you need real clarity of purpose – a deep belief in the value of the difference you will create and, perhaps even more importantly, a belief in what this will mean to you personally, your business and your success. Only if you can see the potential can you expect to be loyal to the power of relationships.

If you are committed to relationships, it becomes natural to be loyal to the people who are involved in them. One of the easiest ways to do this is to apply the Golden Rule:

Do unto others as you would have them do unto you.

If you can do this consistently you create trusted relationships. Others will recognise the fairness of your approach, trust you and naturally reciprocate. Loyalty becomes self-sustaining.

Loyalty is easy when things are going well. What's critical is to remain loyal to others when the going gets tough, or when they are not there. It's at this point that you see whether you continue to act as if they are in the room, or whether you take the opportunity of their absence to talk them down in some way.

People who observe us being disloyal to others, no matter what the reason, may start to believe that we might be disloyal to them too. In a short time, the trust in relationships is broken.

Think of it the other way around: what do you hope people say about you when you are not in the room? And do you trust that they remain loyal?

Consistency is once again vital. Create loyalty in others by demonstrating loyalty yourself, give credit where it is due, and be the first to admit an error and seek to resolve it.

Perhaps this was best described by Jim Collins in his book *Good to Great*, where he described five levels of leadership.[4] As Collins's data-led research demonstrated, the ultimate Level 5 leader (the best) is the one who always looks in the mirror when there is an issue – and always looks out of the window when there is a success.

Ambition

Clarity of ambition, and the courage to pursue it, are fundamental for success at work, but the real pay-off for commitment to relationships sits in the potential that collaboration opens up. A starting point is to be ambitious together.

Imagine a plank of wood between two rocks on a river that just supports your weight as you cross. If you put another plank exactly like it on top you might expect it will support twice your weight. You would be wrong. It will support ten times your weight.

It turns out that 1 + 1 isn't equal to 2; it's much more. And the same thing can be true when two parties approach a relationship based on trust.

Ambition as a behaviour is a willingness to explore potential beyond a specific transaction. It requires openness without any sense of needing to win or compete. It asks you to explore each other's thinking and capabilities, looking for where you can create synergy. The focus is on interdependence rather than one-way service.

This behaviour is the one that drives innovation and creative thinking. It uses the mutual ambition model in Chapter 3 (see p. 74) and fills in the overlap between the parties to identify what they can do together.

Whereas transactional thinking values conformity and is threatened by difference, trust-based relationships value difference as a source of innovation. Or, as the saying goes: "If two people agree, one of them is unnecessary."[5]

Exercise: Working with others to identify the behaviours

How will you apply these behaviours in the context of your specific circumstances, and the relationship you are trying to establish?

What follows will help you and your team, or you with a supplier or customer. It is intended to help you turn these top-level behaviours into real-world interactions. Ideally it should be a joint activity as you answer key questions and document shared behaviour.

On the left-hand side of a whiteboard or flipchart, write down a behaviour principle. Draw two columns to the right of it:

· Things we will do that align to this principle.

· Things we will not do that are at odds with this principle.

Table 2 shows an example of the layout.

Do the same for all five principles. Discuss. Draw conclusions. Write down what you decide.

Where you have an existing relationship, this will flush out behaviours already in evidence that different people see as consistent or clashing with these principles. Discuss and reach an agreed conclusion in a spirit of collaboration and as a way to build trust.

TABLE 2. GO/NO GO BEHAVIOURS

Principle	Things we *will* do that align to this principle	Things we *will not* do that are at odds with this principle
Consideration	*A list of defined behaviours that each party commits to do against each of these principles*	*A list of defined behaviours that each party commits not to do*
Courage		
Honesty		
Loyalty		
Ambition		

This discussion, and the behaviours that you have identified as desirable, are how you have defined your trust relationship. The process establishes a set of shared behaviours for all parties. It reflects both parties being trustworthy, and sets the standards against which character and consistency will be measured.

Although the discussion itself will provide great value, at this stage all you have created are warm words. You are once again at the wedding, looking ahead with a warm glow. Now it is time to turn to the marriage – turning these commitments into consistent, sustained behaviours that are there to help achieve the ambition set out in the clarity stage. The way to do this is to agree intentionally what you will do to manage and govern the relationship so that it can achieve its full potential. That is what the third element of the trust triangle tackles: relationship capability.

5

Capability: the ability to work together

"Talent wins games, but teamwork and intelligence win championships."

Michael Jordan, American former basketball player

Picture a joint venture partnership with a number of major players undertaking a large infrastructure project valued in the billions and taking more than 15 years to complete. The project was not only highly complex but was also going to be affected by many unexpected obstacles, macro and micro economic shocks, unforeseen issues, innovations, and who knows what else. The companies were leaders in their field, including technical experts at the top of their game. There was no question about their capability to provide the services involved.

The question was about their capability to do so together. The project was huge, but the issues thrown up were about the relationship between the people involved which are there whatever the scale of the work. Three years into the project, the joint venture leaders invited us to help them tackle a serious crisis which was costing a lot of money every day and risking on-time delivery.

They had a contract they had hammered out that defined cost sharing, roles and responsibilities, contractual penalties and all the other things that you would find in a megaproject. What was missing was a real understanding of the capability it takes to succeed in a collaborative effort of this kind. It started with exactly what we've already discussed: a lack of time and energy devoted to the clarity of a shared vision and how team members should behave.

What this team needed to do was to have an open and honest discussion about what it meant to be partners – and how they would ensure this would be consistently true of their relationship. This should have involved clarity about each other's roles in the relationship and how they would respond to changes and new demands together, including how they would allocate and manage resources where these were in short supply and often under pressure for potential redeployment on other projects. Because these elements were lacking, so too was the other critical element: something to cement the commitments into a sustainable partnership.

Instead, once the project was won, they had moved rapidly to delivery. One of the many issues that our work helped them identify was that they had not addressed the way the relationship would be led and governed. This is different from project management which, especially in an engineering environment, focuses on the practical deliverables.

They had missed this critical element in their thinking, not budgeted for it, and one of the results was that they were failing to meet each other's needs – for example, about how much money would be earned and when. Instead of collaborating on this, one partner had assumed the role of being in charge and saw the other as a subcontractor.

The knock-on effect was an increasing lack of trust from head offices in the joint venture, because the project wasn't providing the returns it was supposed to. There was also increasingly selfish and defensive behaviour in management meetings as each party responded to pressure from above. In fact, by the time the joint venture leadership engaged us, the only meetings were practical ones tackling technical issues and regularly involving blame and accusations of bad faith. There were no meetings managing the relationship.

This is what is meant by the capability element of the trust triangle: the ability of the parties involved in the trust relationship to achieve outcomes *together*. This story featured a major project involving big companies, but the principles apply in every work environment. In fact, in most cases, smaller organisations and teams have an even higher level of dependence on each other, and so how they govern and manage the relationship is even more critical.

The very minimum that needs to be true for you to be trusted is that you can do what you say you will do and that you do it well. That is true even if it is just a transaction. The aim here is to do far more: to leverage the collaborative power of a high-trust relationship.

The starting point is the acceptance that everyone involved is interdependent.

This is what creates a new capability – the combination of the capacities and resources of all those involved, which will be greater than either party could have achieved. In the clarity dimension it was suggested to set an ambition to make $1 + 1 = 3$ or 33 or 333. In the character dimension, those involved agree the behaviours needed to make that true. The capability dimension involves turning these warm words into consistent action and to be accountable for doing so. It is what the people involved will do to manage the relationship to make sure this ambition is realised.

The two capabilities that build trust

Those involved in a work relationship will usually have some kind of arrangement between them which sets out their respective roles, what is expected or contracted to be done and perhaps what the costs are. There may be a contract of sale or employment, or a partnership agreement.

To go beyond this contractual minimum, you need to treat the relationship as something separate that also needs to be agreed, and to decide how you will manage and maintain it. This defines the capability of the people or organisations involved to establish and maintain a high-trust relationship.

There are two capabilities which turn transaction into trust if addressed intentionally by those involved in the relationship:

1. the way you manage and govern the relationship
2. the way you combine your competencies.

In the joint venture at the start of this chapter, everyone set out an intention to work as partners. But they did not pool

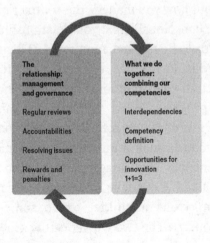

Figure 5: **The capability model**

their resources, continued to act as buyer and seller, and had no structure in place to track their behaviours and develop a high-trust relationship. The result was poor performance. Their relationship had little or no capability except the independent capabilities of the two organisations, which existed in parallel.

The breakthrough comes when you put in place a structure to ensure that high-trust behaviours and actions are present in the work together, and to have consequences if they are not.

Figure 5 shows the elements needed to create that structure. This simple framework applies even if only you are focused on being trustworthy. You can apply these principles to your own way of working to ensure that you are consistent in the way that you (and your team, if relevant) show up, lead and manage relationships, and that you hold yourself accountable for these behaviours.

The relationship: management and governance

The way you manage and govern a relationship will determine whether you continue to trust each other. It's as simple as that. This is not about how you manage the contract or the deal, it is about how you consciously treat your relationship as a separate thing that needs to be tracked, monitored and nurtured.

Governance is, in essence, a formal word for deciding to regularly discuss your relationship rather than outcomes, delivery or process. What gives governance teeth is accountability and consequences for great or poor behaviours.

Simple outcomes may require little governance, but still benefit from consciously managing the relationship to ensure trust is maintained. Let's take an example where a property investor commissions a builder to do some work on an investment property. The two will agree the schedule of works and the price, and there will be some kind of contract between them. But both parties can choose how they work together, and the choice they make will have a real impact when something unforeseen happens, or when there is ambiguity about what to do next.

At the start of the project they can ensure clarity and agree their behaviours – how they will communicate, what feels reasonable, what they will do if and when things go wrong. Beyond that, they can make sure they check in on a regular basis about the relationship, not the job. Both parties can ask some basic questions. Am I doing everything you expect of me right now? Is anything happening that is causing you difficulties? Are you unhappy with me for any reason? Is there anything you need me to do? Are we OK?

This is simple, informal governance, but it so rarely happens. In this kind of situation, most conversations are functional, focused on cost and delivery. Yet if they build trust, and maintain it, then each person will choose to benefit the other. For example, if the builder has other jobs going, they can decide where to send their best plasterer. If the job runs over and therefore the investor is within their rights to withhold funds but the builder needs to finance the next phase, a reasonable arrangement can be made to benefit everyone. Even in this straightforward business arrangement, taking some time to agree how the two parties will work together, checking in that both feel well treated and the relationship is working, will pay dividends, and can ultimately save time and money.

Certainly, the investor will recommend a trusted builder to other investors, and the builder will go the extra mile to work with that investor again. In all situations, individuals working together can agree some key points about how often they will check in with each other on the way they are working together.

In the case of a company providing a mass product to consumers, relationship governance will focus on ensuring they are actively getting consistent feedback and responding to it in a way that builds trust. But more complex relationships, especially between organisations, will need more sophisticated and sustainable governance that does not depend on specific individuals.

A relationship governance checklist

Here are some critical questions to ask when trying to identify the extent to which you'll need a more formal governance process. They are not comprehensive and not all will be relevant to you, but they will serve as a starting point for you and others involved to identify the questions you need to answer to establish a firm structure for a sustainable high-trust relationship.

Which issues do you expect to resolve routinely without reference to other people?

This can be a valuable question as it can empower those working together day to day to sort things out between them, rather than escalating things as a matter of course. Discussing this can reveal surprising levels of tolerance for frontline decision-making, but may also reveal the opposite – that the front line should escalate every variation from the norm. It's important to be clear exactly where the decision-making power lies right from the start.

Where are potential relationship issues raised and resolved?

In many cases it will be valuable to set up a formal relationship management process to ensure regular review of the way the parties work together. This could be a group of leaders together with some of those working on the front line of the relationship.

Where will the leadership team(s) and resources come from?

This may be included in a contractual relationship, but not always. For example, two major departments in a large business decide to develop a relationship agreement to improve collaboration. There may be no existing template for this; it's simply "the way we do things". The value of moving towards a more structured relationship is clear but, if there is cost, who will pay? How will it be led? These may be simple questions, but avoiding doubt and removing guesswork are fundamental principles of this work.

What are fundamental measures that the governance team should report on?

This is about data to measure and ensure outcomes and value. How can you demonstrate the value of collaboration, or the difficulties of achieving it? Here are some relevant questions.

- Is there a process that can be speeded up or simplified with better collaboration?

- Could there be cost savings from removing some processes if the assumption is that the parties trust each other?

- Are there current frustrations which are damaging the relationship that can be solved and therefore make things flow more smoothly?

- Can the value of removing these frustrations be measured?

An example might be between a customer and supplier where slow payments are causing mistrust. Or it might be that the supplier's failure to communicate means that the customer does not know what is happening, and that too causes mistrust.

Simple measurements of payment schedules can show that this is happening and can then be part of the trust conversation.

And are you producing better work as an outcome? This will have real business benefits such as lower costs or pricing, more creative output, higher levels of customer satisfaction, faster to market. Fill in your own objectives here, and it becomes easy to see how better collaboration delivers results. It's important to measure these outcomes, attribute value to the better relationship, and celebrate.

Is the governance of this relationship aligned with the needs of other stakeholders who may need to know how well it is working (e.g. in a contract or partnership)?

As the example at the start of this chapter shows, trust can be damaged because the people involved have not taken into account the needs of other stakeholders, who may put pressure on the relationship as a result.

Think of a head office that expects a certain level of return from a partnership and sees everything through that lens. Openness about this in the relationship will help those involved work out how to manage this situation between themselves and in the way they engage with their respective leaderships. If this is not built into the relationship review, then disaster will strike when those involved come under pressure to deliver margins and cannot discuss it with their partners.

How will this be consistently reviewed together?

Remember that consistency is vital here. The objective is to establish and grow a relationship that builds and maintains trust over time, not just at the start, and so continual reviews of the relationship, based on these governance principles, are critical.

Here's an example from our own experience of what goes wrong if this kind of governance process is not put into place.

A major technology project required multiple suppliers to work together and for them all to work with their client. One of the challenges was that many of the client's staff felt threatened by the project, which would reduce costs.

The suppliers' team members had carved up the work at the bidding stage, but did little or nothing to work on a vision for success (clarity) or to agree how they would behave together (character). The only decision that had been taken was that one company – supplying the hardware – was the main contractor, reporting directly to the client.

Critically, no one had addressed the capability dimension of trust: how the relationships involved would be managed and support the technical delivery of the contract. These relationships included the different suppliers working together and the client and the staff whose co-operation was critical. This is a perfect case of total interdependence between all the people involved, but the style of relationship was contractual and transactional.

Things began to break down quickly. Client staff didn't trust the main supplier – in fact they distrusted the supplier because they thought the supplier was endangering their jobs. As a result, the client failed to supply all the necessary information, let the supplier make false assumptions, failed to engage in meetings and generally behaved badly. But without a governance process that included them, there was nothing to call them out on.

When things started to get worse, the main supplier decided they had to complain and raised it at a senior level. That might have resolved the issue had there been any previous reporting, but instead, they were not believed. The client blamed the supplier for poor delivery and using their people as scapegoats.

Within the supplier team, the challenges involved in this project had an impact on margins. Those involved were not making money. Without a proper governance structure this quickly destroyed trust and engagement. Positions were taken and defended.

The client called a halt to the project.

The sad history of that project is that the client ended up seven years late and tens of millions of pounds over budget. The client's team were on the third round of rework before they sought assistance on how to manage supplier relationships.

There are many lessons to be learned from this project about why relationship governance is so important, and the need to bring all parties to the table. The most important word here is "all": especially where there is scepticism, those whose co-operation is vital need to be in the discussion. The value to be achieved must be co-created; tackling fears, needs and ambitions from the start provides a firm foundation for delivery.

How you hold each other and yourselves accountable

Agreement on what good looks like can be relatively easy. Making sure it remains true is harder. That is why having clear accountability for behaviours and the health of the relationship is critical if this is to stick.

Look at the five principles of behaviour: you will see that honesty is one of them. This is one of the areas where this must be present. Open, honest and straightforward interaction is the basis of trust, even when these are difficult conversations.

Agree at the start that all parties will be accountable for poor behaviours and will act to remedy transgressions. You may want to set out specific ways this will happen, but the truth is that, if you choose to trust each other, you will want to have leeway for bespoke responses to individual situations.

What's important here is of course the word "agreed". The challenge is that in many cases the parties do not agree that something is wrong – or they point the fingers at each other. Leadership teams trying to resolve difficult relationships often see what others are doing wrong but not what they themselves are doing wrong.

Here is the critical point: if there has been a formal decision at a leadership level to build high-trust relationships, and recognition that this is crucial for success, there is real pressure to sort it out based on the principles agreed at the start. Often, having a third party involved to facilitate agreement can be very helpful, so that those involved can have a mirror held up to them to see how they are both behaving and what it feels like from the other's point of view.

But even where this isn't the case, or you are dealing with another individual, openly talking about the bigger picture – which is the need to have trust between you – can be the catalyst for agreement. If you can reach this point, then it is equally important that there is a commitment to accountability, with action taken to tackle the issue and to try and ensure it does not happen again. For this to be a sustained high-trust situation, a sticking plaster to fix the immediate crisis is not the full answer.

If there is no agreement that a high-trust relationship is paramount, then that is useful information that you are in a transactional situation and should act accordingly.

The power of regular review

How often relationships should be reviewed and how that review should take place is another factor in team effectiveness and shouldn't be ignored. In small organisations and teams, a leader may define both how and how often, whereas larger, more autonomous teams may define this as part of a relationship agreement. In any event, a consistent approach is important. Team members need to know that they will be regularly discussing the relationship, not just the activity, and that there is a chance to review how they are working together and whether they are holding themselves and each other to account for the behaviours they defined.

When deciding how and how often, there are various factors to consider.

- Location: are the team members co-located or dispersed?
- Organisational context: do all the team members work for the same organisation; if not, can they participate in the discussion?
- Technology: do the team members have access to virtual meeting capability?
- Phase of work: in the early or critical phases it may be important to schedule more meetings rather than fewer.
- Duration: short sharp and regular reviews tend to be more effective, balanced against avoiding rushed decisions.

Reviewing relationships in this manner is often either overlooked or quickly forgotten about, but if you think about projects or teams that have failed you quickly come to realise that at the heart of it was a failure in relationships. If you talk to the team members, they almost always knew something was wrong but didn't have a way to discuss it and deal with it before it became a critical issue.

How you resolve issues

This is about tackling likely problems right at the start of the relationship and continually looking ahead to any future issues which can be mapped out in advance. In other words, it means seeking clarity about challenges that will be faced and seeking to head them off before they occur.

The chances are that in any working relationship you know the things that could go wrong. You have both been here before. If you are seeking to build trust within an existing relationship, you will already have seen for yourself what goes wrong and this may be why you want to tackle the issue actively. The question of how to resolve issues should be the basis for mapping out and creating a template for what you will do together.

When you do not do this, it can go badly wrong. In our interview with Gregor Craig, when he was CEO and president of one of the UK's biggest construction companies, Skanska, he described a situation where his team were dealing with a customer who had consistently behaved unreasonably (as they saw it). He went in to bat. He got into what he described as an almighty row with the customer, and they had both reached the absolute limits of their patience. He said:

> Then, what do you do? You can walk out of the room. Or you can choose to do something different. We both acknowledged this can't go on. What can be done to fix our relationship? Because, at the moment, it's broken. We don't trust each other.
>
> How do you get to a point where all parties are prepared to trust each other? [1]

This moment led to them sitting down and working through the challenges to deliver what they both wanted – a successful project. The critical point was when they fully understood the problem from each other's perspective.

For the first time they listened to each other and actively sought to see the situation from the other side. They chose trust:

they actively decided to sort things out rather than walk out of the relationship, despite being at the limits of their patience.

Critically, the companies involved had never discussed how they would sort out these issues before this crisis. You do not want to wait until things have got so bad that you have to have a blazing row. It's much better to tackle the potential for this kind of situation up front.

Exercise: What will we do, and when?

If you are to build a high-trust relationship, it is critical to tackle the things that can go wrong together (as well as the great opportunities). Here's what to do.

1. Brainstorm together everything that can go wrong in your relationship.

Don't edit; put everything down on a flipchart or whiteboard. If the teams involved can do this together, so much the better; sharing experiences of the likely challenges ahead will be helpful.

You can't anticipate everything, but you can anticipate things like change, unexpected events, the need to adapt, and problems with personalities.

2. Cluster the challenges into three or four main categories of likely challenge.

These might be categories such as "unexpected change", "cost pressure", "perceived poor delivery by one party" and "new leadership".

3. In each of these categories, write a summary of the most common scenario.

It is likely that the people in the room have been involved in similar projects or relationships before. Sharing a few war stories is a good way to capture the difficulties that are likely to arise and writing these into scenarios.

4. Divide those involved into teams to look at each scenario.

Their task is to set out a clear process to resolve the issue in a way that is consistent with the ambition and governance of the relationship. If the teams have done some of the work outlined earlier in this book – such as setting a clear ambition and being clear about the nature of the relationship – then these conclusions can be used to frame the discussion about how to resolve issues.

5. Review and capture the decisions.

Review these proposals, finalise them to ensure they are consistent with each other, and include them in a relationship agreement. In your regular reviews make sure they are visible and present so that any issues that arise can be resolved.

How you are rewarded or penalised

This aspect of capability is about the trust relationship, not the contract or outcome. In fact, it is important to separate the two, to focus on the relationship as a key element in itself.

Assuming that the different parties are seeking to build trust to achieve some outcome, there are several possible scenarios, shown in Figure 6.

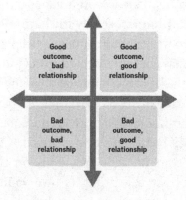

Figure 6: **Outcome vs relationship**

· Both the relationship and the outcome are successful.
· The relationship is poor, but the outcome is successful.
· The relationship is good, but the outcome is unsuccessful.
· Both the relationship and outcome are unsuccessful.

The perfect situation, of course, is if both the relationship and the outcome are successful. A great relationship increases the chance of a successful outcome. Work that is going well helps make everyone happy together. It is a virtuous cycle.

It is completely possible that people or teams who no longer trust each other can continue to deliver together. A supplier contracted to a customer can carry on supplying services even if the relationship has broken down. Two teams in the same business have to work together, whatever the relationship. The challenge is that they will not know what could have been achieved if they focused on trust, though they probably will know the costs being incurred by both sides through the lack of trust. The chances are that they blame each other.

Similarly, teams who trust each other and collaborate well may nevertheless fail. Partners in a major bid might not win; colleagues who have built trust may still have failures. That's life.

In the situation where both the relationship and the outcome are bad, it may or may not be connected. What will almost certainly be true is that the lack of trust contributed to the lack of success.

What does it mean to be rewarded or penalised for our relationship? Simply put: what are the consequences of the way in which trust has been built or destroyed? Can you identify these from the start so that the focus on the relationship is knowing that trust will bring its own value, whatever the outcome of the work together? Similarly, that lack of trust will carry a cost in all circumstances.

Be conscious and intentional about the rewards or penalties for creating trust and be specific about what these are. Doing this at the start of the relationship means everyone is more likely to maintain a long view and tackle short-term issues in the context of the bigger picture. Actively celebrate success; proactively work together on failures.

Here are some scenarios that demonstrate what focusing on rewards might mean.

- Partners who bid together in a highly trusted manner, but lose the bid, are in a much stronger position to bid for future work. This is the reward for putting in the relationship effort – having a much more solid partner with whom to win business.

- The supplier and customer who are just transacting are missing out on the potential value that could be created together. For example, the supplier team may not do any discretionary work for a customer they do not trust; the customer will argue over all the supplier's bills and changes. The chances of them working together on future projects is low.

- A leader who focuses on building high trust from their team will be rewarded with loyalty and better performance. Where loyalty and better performance are missing, it may indicate that there are other issues that need addressing, either by the leader or by individual members of the team. Being clear about the expectation of each with regards to honesty and transparency will underpin the capability of the team and ensure that everyone calls out low-trust behaviours.

- Colleagues who have built high levels of trust may face failure in performance. There are many factors at play. But the reward for having high levels of trust is robustness in the face of failure and ways of dealing with this collaboratively. The penalty – if trust is allowed to break down under this kind of pressure – is that blame and defensive behaviour will dominate and value will be destroyed.

Exercise: What are the rewards and penalties?

Take each of the four reward scenarios, demonstrating the difference between the relationship and the outcome of your work together. Draw on a whiteboard or flipchart the simple box shown in Figure 6.

Use each of these boxes to discuss together what a good or bad outcome is, then what a good or bad relationship is in this context. Write down the value of the good outcome and do the same for the consequences of establishing and maintaining a high-trust relationship, or its opposite.

Write a list of your conclusions beneath the four dimensions in Figure 6: good outcome, bad outcome, high-trust relationship, low-trust relationship. These definitions bring to life the separation of consequences from the work you do to create value and the relationship you build to create it.

It should demonstrate whether the relationship alone has intrinsic value, whatever the outcome. This will spark a discussion about the interplay between these two dimensions of your work together and support the other work you have done in the capability section of your trust building.

What we do together: combining our competencies

The explicit recognition that all value is created together, not simply provided by one party to another, is a major shift in mindset that can provide the foundation for much higher trust relationships – and better outcomes. As has been seen, power-based transactions are inherently weak as the power shifts between different parties, who then leverage that power when they get the chance. Instead, a high-trust relationship starts with a clear understanding of mutuality and synergy.

The question is about collective capability: what will we do to maximise the potential of combining what all parties can do?

Interdependencies

This starts with identifying the interdependencies involved. What do I need you to do in order that I can do what I am supposed to do? And vice versa? This goes back right to the beginning of this book, when the principle of "no guessing" was spelled out.

Interdependencies can be a great destroyer of trust if not fully discussed and understood. This is based on the transactional mindset: if one side is expected to deliver an outcome, and they do not, this results in blame and lack of confidence in them. If they in turn believe they could not do so because the other side did not do what they needed to, then neither side trusts each other, which can lead to conflict.

This cuts across the relationship. When things go wrong, blame inevitably follows. An accountant is paid to provide tax advice, to complete the tax returns for their client and maintain financial order. This is their service, but they depend on the timely and accurate information provided by the client. They also need the client to make decisions, payments and keep their records up to date. The client needs the accountant to give them timely notice of what is required, be proactive in ensuring all deadlines are met and be efficient in their service. If the tax returns are late and the client is fined, there is a high chance they will each blame the other. Trust will be damaged. Clarity about the interdependencies might have avoided that – as long as the behaviours that flowed were consistent with what had been decided.

The chances are that this is a simple discussion: I need you to do this for me so that I can do that. What do you need me to do in order to do your job? Ensuring it is clear, agreed, recorded and followed up will help build trust. Just make sure you are both absolutely clear about what the dependencies are.

Exercise: Mapping interdependencies

In bigger, more complex relationships, this can be tackled through a workshop between the parties specifically on interdependencies. At the centre of the workshop will be a document or whiteboard with four columns drawn on it (if there are two parties involved). Table 3 is a template for what this will look like.

Column 1: *Either* all the key outcomes that the relationship needs to achieve *or* specific tasks that are involved, depending on the nature of the relationship.

Column 2: What party 1 needs to do for this to be achieved.

Column 3: What party 2 needs to do for this to be achieved.

Column 4: Interdependencies.

The exercise is designed to identify any confusion about who is responsible for what, and what each party needs the other to do.

For each outcome or task, get party 1 to kick off with its description of what it believes party 2 needs to do for the outcomes or tasks to be delivered. Make sure party 2 has understood and can describe this clearly.

Then reverse the process: get the second party to go through the list and identify what it sees as the responsibilities of party 1. That in itself will ensure a lively discussion, as there will almost certainly be some misunderstandings or disagreements which can be resolved in the room.

The objective is for both parties to see what the other party believes it needs to do for that outcome or task to happen.

Having agreed who is responsible for what, the parties can identify the interdependencies. For example, if one task needs to be completed by party one before party two can start their task, this sets out the ways in which they need to work together for the outcomes or tasks to be delivered.

TABLE 3. INTERDEPENDENCIES TABLE

Key outcome/task	Party 1	Party 2	Interdependencies

Competency definition

Deciding on what information to fill in has another benefit. Each member of the team is defining their core competencies in the context of the relationship and its shared ambition. I do this, you do that. Core competencies or capabilities explain what each party can do better than the other party. This is the basis of a strong foundation from which the partners will deliver value to customers and stakeholders, seize new opportunities and grow together.

There are many competencies, some of which both parties may feel they have. Any sense of "land grab" or defensiveness is to be avoided if the relationship is to move forward effectively. Easy to say: the objective here is for the person leading the trust building to call this out as an intention at the start of the engagement, and ask everyone involved to highlight any examples of this if they see them.

Here are some core competencies you might recognise.

- Amazon has a logistics capability that has few competitors.
- McDonalds has standardised food production and customer interface that continues to drive growth.
- Ryanair has gone from a start-up to a major carrier by focusing on its core competency of efficiency and low cost.

Exercise: Core competency

As you start thinking about building a business relationship of any kind, ask yourself these fundamental questions.

- What is my core competency or the core competency of my team or business in the context of this specific relationship?
- What value does it create for that relationship?

Opportunity for innovation: 1 + 1 = 3, 33 or 333

In any business relationship, understanding your own core competency and understanding the core competencies of your colleague, partner, client or customer creates a unique opportunity for innovation. Choosing trust allows you to enter a conversation around synergy. In a relationship of trust, new possibilities emerge because the people involved are able to openly share ideas and competencies based on an agreed ambition.

Synergies can arise in many areas. For example, by joining with Pixar, Disney was able to leverage a core competency (advanced animation expertise) that Pixar brought and add that to its own distribution channels and brand that led to massive growth in their combined value. Facebook had failed to create a competency in photo management and upload but, by combining with Instagram which had those competencies, it led to growth for both parts of the organisation, as well as additional capability that neither alone was likely to create.

Not all synergies have to arise from merger or acquisition; they can also arise in partnership. A simple example arose between different suppliers in a major motorway scheme. Each company was supplying significant numbers of people to site.

By agreeing to share transport (and putting both their logos on the doors of the vehicles), they saved tens of thousands of pounds each year on a fixed price contract. What could have been rivalry became synergy.

Looking for synergy can extend beyond suppliers. Customers or clients can also be engaged in core competency discussions and innovation and synergy can flow. Examples include innovative commercial agreements, new product, new market or new service opportunities. The key is to stay alert and to lead with trust in any discussion.

Making it real: the relationship agreement

As we've shown, relying on the contract in business is no basis for a high-trust, high-value relationship.

However, there *is* value in contracting and setting a clear intention right at the start. This applies to the relationship as well as the work. If your relationship is to be based on the trust triangle, then to sustain this you need to be able to refer to a commitment about this shared capability.

The answer is to develop a relationship agreement alongside any other contractual arrangements. This can take many forms, depending on the context, but the principle is a powerful one.

In a relatively small or quick business interaction, this might simply be a discussion at the start about how you will work together, based on the principles here, ideally confirmed by a text or email. For example, if you are collaborating with a colleague on a bid, even an urgent one, at the first meeting spend some time on the elements of the trust triangle. Get clarity on ambition. Agree the behaviours you both expect. Ensure you both understand the interdependencies for the task to be done. Confirm check-ins. This will accelerate progress because you will work better together.

In some cases, an agreement may become part of a commercial or employment contract. It contains all the elements set out in this part of this book, written and agreed. It constitutes a point of reference to be used regularly as part of the governance and review process.

It may take the form of a team charter or team manifesto. The process of putting this together as a team will in itself have value, as you discuss openly the relationship dynamics required to be successful and get buy-in for how you intend as a team to bring to life the commitments you make. This becomes a great reference document for new team members – they know how this team operates and what is expected of them.

It is not our intention here to be too prescriptive about this. The charter or manifesto can take many forms; it can be long or short, and as formal as the relationship itself. It should be a dynamic document, amended and updated as things change. As a guide, Table 4 shows a simple structure that contains the questions that need to be answered.

This agreement can be kept simple, with clear and easily understood statements, but backed up by the more detailed responses to the questions and framework set out in each of the last three chapters.

TABLE 4. A SAMPLE RELATIONSHIP AGREEMENT

Element	What this means
Clarity What we want to achieve together and why	Setting out a clear ambition for this relationship and a summary of how the parties will work together and why.
Character How we will behave together	Using the five principles of behaviour, defined in terms of our exact relationship, what this means in practice. The supporting content can include the different scenarios developed in Chapter 4.

Capability	1. The governance and management of this relationship
What will make this work	A reminder that this sets out the way in which the relationship is reviewed regularly, how the parties are accountable to each other and the process to resolve issues.
	2. Combining competencies
	The relationship agreement may be specific about how the parties will combine their capabilities to achieve their ambition. It may specify commitments relating to interdependencies, innovation, competency and synergy. The supporting documentation should set these out in more detail so that they can be referenced in review meetings.

This agreement is the constitution of the relationship, the manifesto, the charter. Whatever you decide to call it, the work set out here is of no value if it simply creates warm words. What's important is to turn this into real decisions, actions and behaviours, which is why the governance process is so critical.

How does this work in the real world, in situations you will face because of your role and position? That is what Part 3 of this book will now explore.

PART 3

Trust in the real world

This is where the rubber hits the road. How you apply this approach and use the trust triangle in your working life will depend on your role, who you work with and what you are trying to achieve. This section provides practical guidance, exploring what high-trust behaviours look like in different situations.

Once again, there are exercises here to provide practical and varied ways to use the information in your working life. However, we suggest that you adopt the intention and approach that are set out here, use the big ideas as guidance, think about how this applies in your world – and use whichever techniques make sense for your situation.

Take being a leader, for example. There are many different types of leadership situations. You may lead a team, a business, an account or a project. You may lead on a specific function where others require direction from you. Chapter 6 shows why being a high-trust leader will make you more effective in all these situations, and how to apply the trust triangle in a range of leadership contexts.

You may be a team member and want to explore why and how high-trust teams are much more effective. The first question that Chapter 7 asks is: are you really a team with a shared purpose and vision? Tackling this question is an important step to establish high-trust teamwork that enables collaboration, innovation and greater collective performance.

If you work with customers or clients directly, then you are developing business, whether you are selling to them or serving them. Too much business development is transactional, damaging trust, but Chapter 8 shows how to build high trust intentionally with customers and clients so that they choose you and your organisation.

This shows up most starkly in supply chains, where the buying, selling and supply of goods and services is so often based entirely on price and competence. A transformational idea is to approach the supply chain as a collaborative ecosystem, in which trusted relationships are the lifeblood of excellence in a totally interdependent situation. Chapter 9 explores this.

When we talk to each other, we either build or destroy trust. Chapter 10 shows how a high-trust person turns up in conversations. This chapter provides a practical way to ensure you are always building trust, even when conversations are difficult and challenging. This approach will serve you well whatever your role, and in all situations.

6

Being a high-trust leader

"Trust is like the air we breathe – when it's present, nobody
really notices; when it's absent, everybody notices."

Attributed to Warren Buffett, American investor

Leadership is not just about a title. It's about stepping up when
the situation demands it; anyone can find themselves in a
position where they need or choose to lead.

There are many different types of leadership, but they all
have one thing in common: leaders take people on a journey and
therefore in a particular direction. Assuming those people have
choice, they need to trust the person they are following if this is
to work well. Otherwise they'll leave as soon as they can. That is
why being a high-trust leader is so critical to delivering sustained
success – because the people being led can choose to leave your
leadership, or simply stay and not put in discretionary effort. They
can behave transactionally with each other and you. This leads to
people working in parallel, not together, and to functional rather
than active co-operation and teamwork (see Chapter 7).

Or they can remain enthusiastically, work collaboratively
as a team and consistently put in the extra effort to achieve
exceptional outcomes.

The difference is whether or not the leader has chosen trust. It's worth considering how the needs of leadership are changing to explain why this is overwhelmingly the right choice in organisations today.

The changing nature of leadership

In one of the largest research projects of its kind, the business consultancy McKinsey surveyed 189,000 people in 81 organisations about leadership. They studied all the academic literature on the subject. And they considered their own experience in the field.[1]

They decided that four kinds of behaviour accounted for the effectiveness of leaders:

· being supportive
· having a strong results orientation
· seeking different perspectives
· solving problems effectively.

These behaviours might be surprising if you think of a leader in the more traditional way, as someone who commands and controls the people they lead, makes all the big decisions and demands that people follow them. But the McKinsey findings suggest that something very different is needed for the best leaders to be effective.

The overwhelming majority of leadership literature over the past 30 years has pointed in the same direction – away from control and towards consensus. A good question, first posed by management guru John Smythe, is this: are you god or guide?[2]

It's a great question for anyone in a position of leadership. A god issues instructions and leaves those who follow to interpret what they mean. If they get it wrong, the consequences may be disgrace or punishment (though in business, not for eternity).

A guide, however, takes people on a journey with them, and a good guide checks in, consults with those who follow, and often remains flexible on the route but not the destination. The McKinsey leadership behaviours work well in this context.

Leaders are not gods and in a world in which power is more and more dispersed it is an increasingly unsuccessful approach to leadership. Those who follow are rarely in a position where they have to put up with more traditional or poor leadership. In a digital world information is shared and authority questioned.

There are many different models of leadership. One of our favourites was developed by Simon Western, who divided leadership into four styles, or what he called "discourses": the controller, the therapist, the messiah and the eco-leader.[3] He suggested that, although they exist in parallel, they represent the trends in leadership over time, towards the acceptance of complexity and away from a simple command and control philosophy.

The last of these, eco-leadership, sees organisations as ecosystems within ecosystems. Leaders are able to see interdependencies beyond their own organisation or team and see their role as facilitating high-performing networks. They act as a guide. This contrasts with the controller, who sees the organisation like a machine, with employees as functional parts of the whole, and where the focus is on maximising efficiency and optimising productivity.

This aligns with the changing employee demographics. Members of Generation Z (those born between 1996 and 2010) are rapidly becoming the majority of the workforce. All research suggests that they seek purpose and meaning in what they do, continually assess their options and do not see any particular employer or business as being a long-term option for them. They are digital natives who have been trained to know they have choice in every aspect of their lives and are open to many different possibilities and influences.

Think about that quote from Warren Buffett, often considered to be the world's greatest investor. When trust is absent, everybody notices, and the implication is that they act accordingly. Typically, instead of working for the bigger cause, they act for themselves, behave defensively and become sceptical of what they are being told. This is the exact opposite of what a good leader wants to achieve. That's why a good and effective leader has to work hard to be trusted and to maintain that trust.

Exercise: Consider your leaders

Take a moment to consider people who have been your leaders. How much did you trust them? Think just about this issue of trust, not about their competence in other areas.

How did this affect your behaviour and actions?

If you are in a position of leadership, those who follow you will be asking themselves the same question, consciously or unconsciously. Be honest: ask yourself what their answer might be.

If you are unsure about this, find a way to ask them when you're next having a conversation. Ask for honesty and openness, and use this as a way of exploring what you do and say that builds or destroys trust. It can be a very revealing process.

How to be a high-trust leader

As co-founder of the revolutionary ride-hailing app Uber, Travis Kalanick was a digital wonderkid. Founded in 2009 in San Francisco with just three cars for hire, three years later the company was operating in 360 cities in 66 countries. As the company expanded, Kalanick developed a reputation for aggression.

Unfortunately, this extended to the company's workplace, and by 2017, as Uber was dominating the global marketplace, allegations about an aggressive internal culture began to surface. Sexual harassment, bullying and discrimination claims tarnished the company's reputation, which was also facing challenges from regulators around the world. It was said that the company ignored local regulations, failed to treat drivers well and accessed data on them, which was unethical.

Growth, market dominance and shareholder return had become the driving force of the company. Following an investigation in 2017, Travis Kalanick resigned as CEO after pressure from investors, scarred by external boycotts, regulatory criticisms and bad publicity. Drivers and passengers – who were beginning to have more choice – were choosing to leave Uber.

Trust in Kalanick's leadership had collapsed and, with the way the firm had behaved, wider trust in Uber as a positive force in the economy of major cities was also under threat.[4]

Throughout this book, the emphasis has been on contrasting transactional thinking with an approach based on building trust. The move from god to guide is exactly the same journey. The Uber story was one of classic controller behaviour, seeing the organisation as an economic machine with customers, drivers and employees as inputs and with revenue and growth as outcomes. It's a great example of how this can deliver fantastic short-term success but is rarely sustainable because you are dealing with people, who have choice.

A transactional leader offers a deal to those they lead. Many large and successful organisations work in this way. In return for financial reward, colleagues are expected to perform tasks to the best of their ability. Simple. Teams are led on the basis of reward, sometimes linked to success, and the focus is on the task at hand.

In these organisations, there may be no shortage of value and mission statements and purpose declarations. But the reality in many cases is that these are not turned into actual behaviours on a consistent and visible basis.

This is why trust breaks down. Arguably, a leadership that promises a reward in return for work, and delivers it, is demonstrating total trustworthiness. The transactional promise, if honoured, is a demonstration that the leadership can be trusted to deliver.

The challenge is that those promises destroy trust if they don't turn into reality. Few leaders or organisations are honest about their style of leadership and so the disconnect between the words and deeds leads to cynicism, selfish behaviour and blame. It is the foundation of silo behaviour in many organisations, who say they want "one organisation" but reward and recognise individual departments, units or just individuals. The same can apply within a team, even a small one, where the leader behaves transactionally, not in a way that focuses on building trust in themselves, their leadership and in all members of the team.

Deliberately choosing to be a high-trust leader is the basis for *sustainable* success. Applying the principles of the trust triangle will help you decide what this looks like in your own circumstances. This is a high-trust leadership model you can use on the ground.

Clarity

Clarity in leadership is the way you set direction, align your team behind a well understood vision and purpose, and ensure everyone knows what this means in practice. All these elements are important and interdependent.

Samsung is now one of the world's giant technology companies, and one of the leading companies in the South

Korean economy, known as *chaebols*. It began in 1938 as a grocery trading store, and expanded after the Korean War, helped by a deliberate strategy by the government to modernise and industrialise the country. Its focus was on a range of industries, including textiles and shipbuilding, and it only entered the electronics market in 1969.

When its founder, Lee Byung-chull, died in 1987 he was succeeded by his son, Lee Kun-hee. Lee Kun-hee's leadership has been instrumental in the rise of Samsung to become one of the world's great companies and brands and a global technology leader.

In the early 1990s, soon after taking over, he launched his New Management initiative, which marked a turning point in Samsung's history.[5] It's a great example of clarity as a foundation for effective leadership. At the time, Samsung was facing challenges related to product quality, which affected its reputation and competitiveness in the global market. In 1993, Lee Kun-hee convened a three-day executive meeting in Frankfurt in Germany, and called for a radical change in the company's approach and culture.

He famously told Samsung executives: "Change everything except your wife and children." With these words, he sent a strong message that Samsung needed to undergo a complete transformation, from its corporate culture to its product development processes, and focus on quality.

In 1995, he sent an even stronger signal on quality. He gathered 150,000 faulty mobile phones manufactured by Samsung and ordered them to be destroyed in a massive bonfire in front of the company's headquarters.

The New Management initiative was a call for innovation, quality and customer-focus. Lee Kun-hee demanded that employees challenge the status quo and embrace change. He urged them to think outside the box, take risks, and invest in research and development to create cutting-edge technologies and products. He had set a direction and then empowered his colleagues to act on this.

He had at the centre of his philosophy ideas that are echoed in this book: change comes when we trust each other, walk the right path, don't drag others down, and don't be afraid of criticism.

Under this new vision, Samsung shifted its focus away from low-cost manufacturing and pursued a strategy of developing high-quality, premium products. The company invested heavily in R&D and made strategic acquisitions to gain access to advanced technologies. It sought to become a leader in various technology sectors, including semiconductors, displays and mobile phones.

The effects of the New Management initiative were fundamental. Samsung became synonymous with innovation and excellence, gaining recognition for its high-quality products and pioneering technologies. Today, its Galaxy range of mobile devices vies with Apple's as the best-selling smartphone in the world.

Lee Kun-hee's bold and transformative approach remains a testament to the power of visionary leadership in reshaping the destiny of a company and leaving a lasting impact on the industry. It's a lesson to all leaders that clarity of direction, and alignment behind this vision, is critical.

Clarity is a cornerstone of the trust triangle because, without it, no one is quite sure what is expected of them and so acts according to their own interpretations. The result is misalignment, different people pointing in different directions and poorer performance. Trust is destroyed as those in charge get frustrated by their teams for not doing what they had expected, and feel they cannot rely on them in the future. This can lead to command and control management, with the results set out at the start of this chapter.

When we have worked with boards to help them build high trust within senior teams, our starting point is to interview individual members and ask them very simple questions, such as these.

- What value do you create for your customers?
- How are you special, different or great?
- Who exactly are your most important customers?
- What are the three key elements of your strategy?
- Can you describe for me what you sell?

There are always startling variations in the responses, and sometimes individuals struggle to answer questions convincingly. So, at a senior leadership level, even at board level, there will be a lack of alignment around some fundamental issues.

The result is that, when they discuss and decide on business issues, these individuals are looking at them through different lenses. This leads to tactical decision-making which may not be consistent with any overall strategy, and different members of the leadership will view with alarm what colleagues are doing. Leaders will secretly no longer trust fellow members who have made recommendations that come from an entirely different set of priorities. That leads to a destruction of trust, which then causes self-centred behaviour and blame.

So the first task of high-trust leadership is to achieve clarity on the fundamentals, and ensure that everyone in the team understands what this means in practice. It is about setting an ambition for the team you are leading which is exciting and true – and has been developed with their help.

This is true at every level of leadership. Even if you find yourself in a temporary situation where you need to lead, having everyone clear and aligned is critical if you are to retain their trust – and to be able to trust them as part of the team.

Chapter 4 explored the importance of clarity for trust. This chapter will consider how to apply the principles outlined there in the context of leadership.

Who will benefit, and why?

Leadership has to have a purpose. Your team, organisation or partnership is working together to deliver a service, product or outcome that will have an impact on other people specific to your situation, whether customers, colleagues, patients, citizens, partners, business people or consumers. You need to be specific and clear about exactly who will benefit and therefore choose (if they have a choice) to use your service or product.

There will usually be multiple answers to this question. Think about the most important groups – perhaps the biggest customers, or the business-critical parts of the organisation you serve – and try to group them into useful categories. Think about how this makes the most sense. Categorising them in terms of size, for example, may or may not be the most valuable method. Instead, putting them into types of need, or strength of relationship, or job description of the decision-maker involved, may be a better approach. It takes time to decide which type of categorisation is most useful, but it is time well spent.

Clarity and agreement on who these people are will help to make sure everything you do as a team or organisation is focused on meeting their needs and desires. Starting with "them" not "us" sets the tone for everything that follows.

The second part of this question is to develop a clear sense of their "why".

- What is their motivation for engaging with what your team or organisation does?
- What benefits accrue to them as a result?
- What do they care about most?

Working hard on these two questions can be the best way to set a powerful and exciting ambition for the people you lead. It frames your work together in terms of ultimate outcome, and aligns the team behind a clear sense of what you want to achieve together.

Let's say, for example, you lead a cancer unit in a hospital. When you consider who you serve, the first thing that leaps out is that they are the people of a specific geography, making your ambition highly relevant to those in your team who probably also live locally.

Consider the groups. Rather than dividing them into types of cancer, think about other more useful categories to align the team's efforts. For example, those who have to come into hospital as in-patients, those treated as external patients, and those at different stages of treatment.

Consider too the other critical people you serve or work with: relatives of patients, other medical units, wider community bodies, national institutions. Mapping these out into categories helps provide clarity for teams who have to balance different demands and priorities.

Simplify this set of categories as far as you can. For example, you might have patients and their families at four different stages of treatment, as well as hospital colleagues, local external stakeholders and national external stakeholders.

Consider what each of these groups cares about and why. By discussing and clarifying this, you will begin to see patterns and commonalities. For example, themes could be "being well informed", "highest quality care" and "feeling compassion". These begin to identify some of the elements that are most important to your ambition as a team.

It is also the start of clarity as a foundation for trust. Mapping this out and sharing the results as part of your strategy will ensure that those who work on the front line with each of these different groups will have a clear idea of what the whole team has decided is the ambition for that category of people. For example, if the ambition includes a focus on treating everyone as an individual, then this becomes a core part of what frontline staff should demonstrate and their leaders must enable. Everyone is clear that this is seen as important to the whole team.

What value are you creating?

This may be a strange question when asked of an internal team, but it's a powerful one. It captures how you respond to the needs identified by question 1: who will benefit, and why? When value is co-created, everyone involved is interdependent. As the leader of a team, it is important that everyone understands the value you create collectively for the people you serve, and what makes your team special, different and great. This is not just about individual jobs being done well.

Your job is also to ensure this remains true, and that you get even better in each of these areas. If you and your team are unsure about who will benefit, and why, this is the basis for misalignment of expectations and destruction of trust for all the reasons already explored. This is different from a task list. It's an exploration of *how* you do what you do, the ways you and your team want to show up consistently, and the value you provide to answer the "whys" from your stakeholders.

Let's return to the cancer unit. The obvious, functional

answer to asking "why" in this case might be something like: to treat cancers in our community as well as possible and with the best possible outcomes. This is fine as far as it goes, but it's not especially inspiring or distinctive.

Exploring the "whys" of the different groups of beneficiaries can help to create something more specific and dynamic. Ideas might include: "healing people in (our town) so that they go on to live great lives", "being a pillar of excellence in the community" or "providing world-class cancer care for our community". As these ideas become refined, the task then is to define what they mean in practice.

For example, what is world-class cancer care on a day-to-day basis? If you have divided the patients into cancer stages, what does it look like at each stage? Creating clarity about the outcome of the team's work like this means everyone is clear about the collective ambition. This eliminates ambiguity, and with it the risk that trust falls through the cracks between perceptions. If I provide world-class cancer care in my role but you fail in yours, consistency is lost in our relationship and trust between us breaks down.

How will you work together?

This question is about defining the framework of the relationships in your team. The behaviours involved will be addressed below, but it is important to establish the exact nature of the relationships in relation to the outcomes the team is expected to achieve.

Imagine you lead a technology service delivery team. Your responsibility is to delight the customer, but to do so at a healthy profit. The members of your team know that this is important, but they work on the front line with the customer and consistently do much more work than is being paid for.

Their motivation is good – they want to delight the customer, whom they meet daily. But they feel less responsible for the profitability of the contract, which they see as your job. As a result, the project is less profitable because their time costs money.

There may be clarity of ambition here but not of the authority, responsibilities and the way in which this team will work collectively to achieve the outcome. One way to deal with this is simply to demand that they behave in a strictly contractual way or face the consequences. This is an exertion of power that will damage your relationship with them and theirs with the customer. It will be a short-term fix.

A better way is to ensure there is clarity about the collective responsibility to achieve the outcome of a delighted customer *and* a profitable contract would be to explore with the team how you work together to achieve this. As leader you set the ambition and are clear about what the outcome has to be. But the way you work together to achieve this can be developed between you, subject to your final agreement (and potentially that of others, such as the customer or your boss). It is important that these behaviours are clear and well understood. The way in which you tackle issues like this will be as important as what you decide, and will help build trust.

Exactly the same principles apply in all leadership situations, whether this is a board of a company or a small start-up. Being clear on responsibilities, authority and how you will work together sets the framework for what follows – the behaviours you demonstrate and expect from the team.

Character

Behaviours are where trust is so often damaged, almost always inadvertently. Often when people are at work, they behave in the way that they think that position demands rather than how they would choose to be in their own lives. Usually unconsciously, they put on the professional clothes of their job and become someone else.

The result is that they lose authenticity. They try to be someone they are not, and at some point this becomes obvious. The mask slips. This damages trust in their leadership. They may still be able to exert power, but they lose authority. The answer, of course, is to be authentic. To be more human. To be more yourself. To be consistent.

Paul Polman successfully led the global business Unilever for ten years, and did so with a focus on sustainability. On leaving the firm he co-wrote the book *Net Positive*, and he says: "We've all done a good job of divorcing our personal selves from work life, but at a high cost. We believe that a business is and should be human with real people serving the needs of other real people."[6]

It was the character and behaviour of Travis Kalanick and Uber that destroyed trust in his leadership and, to some extent, in the company. Not the other dimensions of trust – its capability or the clarity of its mission.

How leaders behave will determine the experience of the people they lead and influence their behaviours. Those behaviours will determine the culture of that group of people. People do as you do, not as you say, because that is deemed to be the way to progress. They will be looking to you for cues about how they too should act.

As a leader, think carefully about how your behaviours affect and influence your colleagues. Make conscious, intentional decisions, rather than falling prey to knee-jerk responses to situations and challenges. Consider how you choose to respond to situations as a human being, with your character and personality, and make this part of your decision-making about what to do next and how to do it.

If these behaviours are clear and consistent, trust is built and maintained. If they are not, trust is destroyed. This will be critical to the success of the team involved.

A vital task of a leader is to achieve the ambition (set out at the clarity stage) through the actions and behaviours of those they lead. The actions required will change over time and will depend on what happens, but the behaviours should be consistent and well understood.

Chapter 5 outlined the importance of an agreed set of behaviours. The five principles of behaviour are a good foundation: consideration, courage, honesty, loyalty and ambition.

A leader and their team are able to develop their own version of this in a way that works for them. Using these five or similar behaviours as a guide moves you away from more traditional, power-based models of leadership. A high-trust leader consistently behaves with their team in a way that focuses on relationships as well as tasks and holds themselves and each other accountable for maintaining them – in bad times as well as good.

Take, for example, the principle of consideration (fairness). Let's look back at the questions outlined in Chapter 4.

· What are you hoping to achieve?
· What would success for you look like?
· Who else is involved who has an interest in success?

These questions are not only relevant when building high-trust relationships with sales prospects or customers. They are also a powerful device for engaging colleagues or a potential new hire. With a customer you are exploring how a service or product might meet their needs and ambitions. Start with the same intent with colleagues and team members.

The principle of mutual value also applies to the people you lead. The team has an ambition to fulfil, and so the task of leadership in this context is to determine what each team member (or potential recruit) contributes and how their ambitions can be realised in the context of what you need to achieve together. The key elements of collaboration and interdependence are as true within a team as they are between an organisation and its customers or partners.

Bear in mind that the principles are all geared towards success and performance. For example, consideration is not just about treating people fairly, important as this is. It's also about fairness to the whole team and others who depend on its performance.

A leader will inevitably have to make decisions that are not always popular with everyone. But if these decisions are reached in a way that shows consistency with core principles, involving those being led as much as possible, trust can still be maintained. This is the essence of guide-based rather than god-based leadership.

Capability

The capability model in Chapter 5 is a high-trust way to effective leadership. It's a powerful leadership framework. As before, the level of formality around this framework will depend on your own context and situation. If you lead a team, if you are a CEO leading senior executives or the chair of a board, you may need a more formal process and approach.

But the principles contained here are useful questions to explore with those you lead in any situation so that you build trust capability between you. They can be dealt with quickly, as relevant, as long as there is clarity about the answers, ideally with a contribution from everyone involved.

A good starting point for each of these questions is for you as a leader to answer them for yourself. For example: how would you like to govern team relationships? How would you like to resolve issues that arise? How, and how often, should you meet to discuss how relationships are working? Remember, this is not governing the delivery aspects of the team, but the relationships of those in it, including the relationships with you as leader.

The exercise on interdependencies (p. 120) works very well in a leadership context. It provides a framework for a discussion about the interdependencies in the team or organisation so that everyone involved has a chance to discuss this fully and align. In some situations, the leader may need to adjudicate to reach a decision. As long as the process has been seen to be consultative and fair, then this is reasonable. The aim is to provide clarity to everyone so that they can trust that others see the interdependency in the same way.

Use your own conclusions as the start of a conversation with your team to iterate the answers with their contribution. Ultimately, the job of leadership is to ensure decisions are made; that is your role in this process, but the way you reach that decision is as important as the decision that is reached.

If you have worked through the five principles of behaviour, these will be an important guide, and the capability stage of this work is to capture and formalise the decisions reached. For example, if you have looked in detail about what being honest with each other means in the context of real situations you are likely to face, then using this as part of the way you want to resolve issues is powerful. If everyone is expected to be honest with each other, there is no excuse for people to avoid tackling tough challenges with each other or the team, safe in the knowledge that this is the right kind of behaviour provided they do so in a way that is consistent with the principles of consideration and loyalty.

This is in line with the principle of what business writer Patrick Lencioni called vulnerability-based trust in his book *The Five Dysfunctions of a Team.*[7] It's one of the most powerful energies in a team because, if it is present, it means individuals can express perceived weaknesses and ask for help, confidently put forward ideas that may not fly but will not damage their position or be shot down, or share challenges they face personally or professionally. They can trust that others will not exploit their vulnerability.

For Lencioni, the critical factor is for the leader to share vulnerabilities and demonstrate that it's all right to do so. Comments such as: 'I don't know the answer to this,' "I'm struggling to tackle this problem", or that express emotion such as: "I was really scared when this happened," show the team that everyone is human and that showing vulnerability is a supported behaviour.

In the process of tackling the capability questions, this kind of conversation can support the development of a shared team culture. It may be fundamental to the way issues are resolved that those involved can share weaknesses in the expectation that the team will rally round and help. If they do not, this should be called out by the leader as inconsistent with the relationship that has been agreed and those involved can be held accountable for that behaviour.

By demonstrating commitment to the principles agreed, leaders build higher trust in their leadership and the whole team can work together more effectively, knowing that the way they interact has been agreed and is consistent. There may be some people who cannot work in the way that has been agreed, which may be a reason for them to leave the team; those who remain demonstrate their trust and loyalty to the culture they've agreed with their leader.

A high-trust leader establishes a high-trust culture with those they lead. A low-trust leader does the opposite. In an age when command and control leadership is out of step with a rapidly changing business environment and people's expectations, trust-based leadership offers a model that can help you to adapt and respond quickly and flexibly by working collaboratively with team members to achieve team goals.

7

More effective teamwork

"If you want to go fast, go alone. If you
want to go far, go together."

Proverb

As Apollo 13 headed for the moon in April 1970, disaster
struck. It required a radical change in mindset from the NASA
scientists involved to solve the problem, and it was one of the
greatest ever examples of teamwork in action.[1]

Just 56 hours into the mission, the spacecraft suffered a
catastrophic explosion in the command module (the main part
of the spaceship that transported the crew to and from the
moon), which destroyed its ability to fire its engines or provide
life support to the crew. The lunar module, designed to be an
independent spacecraft for its final descent to and ascent from
the lunar surface, became their lifeboat.

But it was designed to support two men, not three. On top
of that, the carbon dioxide scrubbers were becoming exhausted
and the crew were at serious risk of dying from carbon dioxide
poisoning. It was at this point the ground team realised that the
replaceable carbon dioxide scrubbers in the command module
were square and those in the lunar module were round. They
didn't match.

Back on earth, the ground controllers rigged up a copy of the lunar module to work out what to do. They confronted the challenge with the call to action which has become legend: "Failure is not an option!"[2]

This monumental effort in teamwork was ultimately successful. Gaffer tape, covers from flight manuals, plastic bags and suit hoses were put together and a series of detailed instructions were drawn up. This enabled the flight crew to recreate the work of the ground-based teams, which saved them from dying.

So what qualities did this extended team, both on the ground and in the stricken craft, have that saved the day?

- Clarity. All members of the team had complete clarity about what they were trying to do, by when and the result they had to achieve.

- Character. The team defined a leadership role and opted to use brainstorming as their preferred behaviour. They abandoned the existing silos and divisions between functions. Every approach was considered equally until the team jointly agreed the best outcome. Jobs were decided based on skill set, not seniority.

- Capability. The team consisted of skills from many different aspects of the engineering and other teams. This combination of skills was critical to the collaborative approach they took – total interdependence. The governance of the team was based on face-to-face discussion and a careful eye on progress against the clock.

This high-performing team had no choice but to trust each other to address a critical problem and succeed. They had to collaborate and do so with a clear, focused and agreed objective. Every team that wants to achieve its own goals should model itself in the same way.

You will recall Patrick Lencioni's idea that vulnerability-based trust is an essential character trait for high-trust teams. Think about what might have happened if this had not been in place here. If the Apollo 13 team had wasted its efforts trying to blame the designers for making different shape scrubbers and find out who made this "blunder", to apportion blame, they simply wouldn't have been able to maintain the same team ethos. Time would have been wasted, and the outcome might have been different.

The members of great teams trust each other. And they produce better outcomes by communicating more powerfully, problem-solving more effectively, using resources more efficiently, learning and innovating faster, and engaging employees more effectively.

Creating a high-performing team

If the objective is a high-performing team, trust is the important foundation. The rest of this chapter lays out how to use the trust triangle to build a high-trust team.

Clarity

The first task is to be sure you are a team.

It should be straightforward to bring together a team with a single ambition. Where the members sit within one part of a business, it can be straightforward. For example, a sales team working for one sales leader should have individual goals that align, and therefore agreeing a shared ambition or vision for the team should be relatively simple.

In these cases, a leader may accept that they are leading a "group" not a real "team". In a group the overall goal is met by the sum of the individual contributions, not via shared effort towards a common goal. In a group people might communicate differently to those in a team – individual progress will be more important than the overall goal, and performance tables might be in common use. Groups often exhibit competitive rather than collaborative behaviours.

There are lots of examples where this is true. A project team consisting of colleagues or contractors may really be a group of people focused on their own needs and obligations within the project, and what they can get from it. In most law firms, for example, the different partners trade under the same name but are focused on their own billing and clients. A customer and its suppliers need to work closely together but fail to collaborate. Think of how this applies in your own situation, where what is called a "team" is in fact a "group".

Successful group members, rewarded for their individual contributions, would rather not share with other members how they succeed because it might threaten their own position. In many environments, it's common for the most successful group member to be promoted to lead a similar group. This reinforces the belief among members of the group that they need to compete and have sharp elbows to progress.

Trust within groups is very different to trust in teams. Trust in groups tends to be at a personal level but may turn into active competition in a business context. Individuals within a group may like each other, socialise and interact freely outside work, but fail to be open and honest, or simply withhold information that may erode their own competitive advantage they see as important to individual success. The result is the absence or erosion of trust between colleagues.

It's important to assess whether you are leading or are part of a group or a team. Use the following table to assess where you, and the people you are working with, sit. Group or team?

TABLE 5. GROUP OR TEAM?

Group	Team
Individual accountability	Individual and mutual accountability
Come together to share information and perspectives	Frequently come together for discussion, decision-making, problem-solving and planning
Focus on individual goals	Focus on team goals
Produce individual work products	Produce collective work products
Define individual roles, responsibilities and tasks	Define individual roles, responsibilities and tasks to help the team do its work. Often share and rotate them
Concerned with one's outcome and challenges	Concerned with the outcomes of everyone and the challenges the team faces
The leader shapes purpose, goals and approach to work	The team leader shapes purpose, goals and approach to working with team members
The leader dominates and controls the group	The leader acts as a facilitator
The leader leads and conducts meetings	Team members actively participate in the meeting discussions and eventual outcomes
The leader usually assigns work to the members	The team members decide on the disbursements of work assignments
Groups do not need to focus on specific outcomes or a common purpose	Teams require the coordination of tasks and activities to achieve a shared aim
Individuals in a group can be disconnected from one another and not rely on the other members	Team members are interdependent because they bring to bear a set of resources to produce a common outcome
Groups are generally much more informal. Roles do not need to be assigned, and norms of behaviour do not need to develop	Team members' individual roles and duties are specified, and their ways of working together are defined

When you have thought about this, don't be surprised if the answer points towards being a group rather than a team. So much of our corporate culture is embedded in transactional thinking, with competition seen as the route to success, that many "teams" are more accurately "groups".

Now you have decided what you currently are – a team or a group – it's important to decide whether this is the best structure for your needs and those of your organisation. The question is how you achieve trust with and across a group or team. Leaders can do so with group members on a one-to-one basis, but without taking full advantage of the benefits of a properly defined and functioning *interdependent* team.

That's why this chapter considers trust in teams rather than groups. It may also help you turn a group into a team, if that is what you decide to do.

A team without shared clarity is no team

Try this exercise with your colleagues or team. Ask them to stand up and clear a space around themselves. Get them to close their eyes and to turn around three times on the spot with their eyes closed, if they feel safe to do so. Keeping their eyes closed, ask them to point to where they think North is. Unsurprisingly, they will point in many different directions. Now suggest they open their eyes and put their best effort into heading wherever they think is North.

They all have different perceptions of which way they need to go. They are all convinced about which direction is correct, and wonder why others aren't following the same course.

This can also be true when their eyes are open throughout the exercise.

Too many teams struggle because they lack clarity. In some cases, it's because the leadership of their organisation simply fails to provide clarity and team members lack the courage to seek it. You might have experience of a business where the leadership sets a growth goal and the key rationale for that goal was what happened or what didn't happen last year.

Without clarity about how to grow, what to do, what to

stop doing, what's a priority, when we need to do it by, well intentioned teams do their best and end up failing, pulling in different directions and frustrated. In building a shared vision and strategy a good leader who trusts their team sets direction and shapes its thinking so that each member is clear and committed to the outcome. Team members then have a responsibility and opportunity to influence and shape how they behave and the outcomes. This may take more time and dialogue up front, allowing for debate, challenge and discussion, but the outcome in terms of clarity and commitment more than repays the investment.

To illustrate how shared clarity can help an organisation, consider Netflix and how it engaged its team to create and deliver a new strategy. Because of its clear focus – to provide home entertainment in a way that gives the consumer choice – it was able to create an environment where diversity of thought and creativity could flourish.

Netflix had built its business as a DVD rental service but, like VHS rental before it, it could see that there would be a short life for this latest physical format. Its decision to pivot towards becoming the streaming giant and content creator we know today had great teamwork at its heart.

The company encouraged employees to engage in open and honest discussions and collaborate on key decisions in open meetings where diversity was valued and different inputs were sought.[3] This contrasts starkly with many traditional organisations where some team or group is responsible for "innovation" or "design" or "product engineering" and they come up with ideas to be considered by senior leadership.

The Netflix approach ensured that the company was able to move its strategy not just once, but also by constantly adapting to changing market conditions. This led to its most significant changes – for example, moving into a streaming market, and becoming a content creator rather than just a provider. These were massive and highly innovative decisions by the company, which required huge investment of time, people and money. This inclusive and collaborative culture has been key to Netflix being able to innovate and stay ahead of its competitors in a rapidly evolving industry.

Netflix's successful move into original content production also demonstrates the value of teamwork in driving strategic success. By involving employees from various departments in the decision-making process and encouraging collaboration, Netflix has been able to create a diverse range of content that appeals to a wide audience, ultimately solidifying its position as a global leader in streaming entertainment.

When you have an intent to engage people in a team, building shared clarity is relatively simple. As a leader you may have a view of what the team needs to achieve, perhaps handed down from more senior teams or leaders. Your role is to share that goal with the team and to make sure that everyone has complete consistency in understanding.

A last word on clarity. As a leader who chooses trust, you must remember to check not only that your team is committed to the vision, but that the vision also works for other stakeholders. This can be critically important when trying to build cross-functional teams in what may have been a typical siloed organisation. If, say, you want sales, marketing, human resources and operations to sign up for a new project, don't get tripped up by their bosses putting a halt on their engagement because it's not aligned with their needs. Your role is to help them to align and engage proactively with each other as stakeholders, an example of the consideration behaviour in action (see Chapter 4).

Character

It's easy to assume that people who work for the same company naturally behave in the same way. The reality is that most companies fail to set clear values that determine behaviour, and rely on informal norms of behaviour and an employee handbook to police what happens. These are guide rails that leave too much to chance, and fail to bond a team, especially when that team is faced with a tough situation or difficult decisions.

Character – defining team behaviours – is worth far more investment of time than it is typically afforded if the team wants to continue to thrive when the going gets tough.

When you define these behaviours it's important to test them with examples, or "what ifs". Make sure all the team members have a chance to test their examples and experiences to create clarity, common definition and shared examples of how the behaviours will apply. Most important is to think of potentially difficult scenarios and ask: "How will these behaviours apply when times are tough?" or, equally important: "How will these behaviours apply when personal priorities change?"

Only by being honest about all the difficult times and building what you might think of as a war-room approach does the team build confidence that this intent to work collaboratively will stand the test of time. Trust is established.

Remuneration and its impact on trust in teams

As you think about your behaviours as a team, make sure you take personal and team remuneration and reward into account.

One team we advised drew on the skills of marketing, sales, and learning and development to support a strategic goal in new market development. Everybody signed up enthusiastically to being part of the team and the behaviours that were expected of them, and they believed they could participate fully while still achieving their own goals in the rest of their responsibility. The reality changed with the market downturn they experienced.

The team's sales remuneration plan emphasised the achievement of revenue goals in a financial year. As time went on it became clear to some of the sales people that they were going to miss their personal goals and they started to give less and less time and effort to the strategic project. This breakdown in agreed behaviours had a significant impact on trust and the willingness of others to give their efforts to this kind of project in the future.

Failing to explore the impact of remuneration (and recognition) on behaviours can lead to a breakdown in trust. It's vital to understand that money (and other recognition) talks, and to ensure that the ambition and goal for the team supports their personal goals. It is also important to explore what behaviours you will deploy if these goals start to become challenging.

Teamwork and trust can be enhanced by remuneration. For example, one team adopted a remuneration process that was based on personal and team rewards. Everybody was given a bonus for achieving their individual goal, but the bonus for individuals who met their individual goals went up substantially (it more than doubled) when the team also achieved its goal. This had the impact of focusing everyone on giving their best, while also supporting each other in contributing to the wider team goal. They all realised it would be much easier to achieve their bonus if each member contributed well rather than leaving it to a few to carry the burden. Working as a team like this encouraged collaboration, honesty and innovation – all of which led to increased trust and engagement.

Capability

Investing time, people and money into a team is a conscious choice. Resources aren't infinite and if team members are to be trustworthy and to trust each other it's vital that they know what they are getting into. It's also critical that they manage the relationship with other team members in a way that they all understand and that reflects the peer-to-peer relationship of trust-based teams.

Critical questions of capability

To be trustworthy you must understand yourself and the skills and capabilities you have or can acquire that are important to the team achieving its ambition. Take a moment and consider the following.

· What are you or your team really good at?

· Which of those skills and attributes can you honestly say you are willing to invest into the team?

The risk to many teams and their trust in each other is when participants either overestimate their capability, or land-grab areas of responsibility out of ego. People who are focused on a "need" to be the leader, for example, will alienate and cause others to distrust them if it quickly becomes clear that others have more appropriate skills.

Your role here is to be honest and transparent with others about how you have arrived at your personal assessment. Remember the behaviours of consideration and courage. Be considerate of others' views, listen to their beliefs and have the courage to accept when your opinion needs to change.

This isn't simply about compromise. Trust isn't built in teams by agreeing to have someone in a role simply because they are the least bad option. High-trust teams need to acknowledge when a capability that's critical to success is needed and develop a plan together for how it will be acquired.

Governance in high-trust teams

Over and above the formal business guidelines and rules in an employee handbook, the best teams have an agreement about how they will manage their relationships. Chapter 5 discussed the value of a relationship agreement in which the team captures its commitments in terms of the dimensions of the trust triangle. This is often known as a team charter or team manifesto, and its format is less important than the commitment to set out how this will be a real team with high levels of trust and an agreed culture.

This makes a real difference because it captures and measures behaviours as well as outcomes. This issue of measurement, and therefore accountability, is critical.

A trust-based team that commits to measuring behaviour needs to:

- check that the agreed behaviours are in evidence
- celebrate and communicate where behaviours are in evidence
- modify behaviour where necessary to improve trust and teamwork
- highlight and resolve behaviour gaps.

To do this, resources need to be invested by the team in collecting, disseminating and celebrating agreed behaviours and how they link to the outcomes the team is achieving.

This focus on behaviours is critical. A focus solely on outcomes can lead to behaviours that destroy trust in teams; the need to "win" and achieve the objective outweighs an intention to demonstrate consideration, courage, honesty, loyalty and ambition. Short-term wins can mean the long-term death of the relationships that bring the benefits of trust to teams.

In summary, high-trust teams have the potential to increase communication, collaboration, problem-solving, innovation, employee engagement and create greater commercial success. This is what every team leader wants. Choosing trust can create an environment where this is achieved.

8

Trust-based business development

"The best way to find out if you can trust
somebody is to trust them."

Ernest Hemingway, American novelist

Clayton Christenson, author of *The Innovator's Dilemma*,[1] shared an excellent example of how the same type of product can have a very different value proposition depending on different target markets: milkshakes. He looked at two manufacturers, one of whom created thick, fruit-laden milkshakes, while the other made thinner, sweet milkshakes. The two manufacturers developed these variations on a theme because they saw that different markets would value the differences they created.

The thick milkshake was designed for a modern commuter or office worker. Many of them didn't have time for a nutritious breakfast but had time on their commute. As a result, they were hungry during the morning and tended to eat products that were less healthy. They were spending a lot of money on snacks. The value of the thick milkshake was as a nutritious, healthy alternative to snacking by being a breakfast on the go. The thin milkshake was aimed at parents who wanted to give their children a relatively healthy treat that was also quick and easy to consume, while providing vitamins and supplements too.

As you think about the different markets these two similar products supported, you can quickly see that each requires a very different narrative to define it. Creating this level of clarity is the first step to thinking about others' priorities and starting to build a relationship with individuals, businesses and even markets as a high-trust basis for business development.

It's also worth thinking about your intent towards your customers or clients and whether they are predisposed to trust you.

Business development has long suffered from low trust between potential customers and the salespeople whose livelihoods are dependent on their business. But moving from a transactional sales process to a collaborative approach that builds trust will improve results for both parties. There's real value in this: Deloitte research showed that customers who trust a brand are 88% more likely to buy it again.[2] In a sea of widespread distrust, this is a way to stand out from the crowd.

But let's start with a key question. Do business development people and their customers and clients generally trust each other? And if not, why not?

The reality is that trust is often lacking in business development because an overwhelming majority of salespeople are driven by the short-term transactional goals set by their organisations. For them to succeed, the only logical position they can see is to operate out of self-interest. Although they may not be dishonest, what they tend to do is to convince their potential buyers that whatever they're selling will meet the customer's needs whether there is a good fit or not. Talk to these decision-makers and the most common complaint they have is that "they seemed to know what I needed without even asking me, and funnily enough it was what they had to sell".

It's the old adage that if all you have is a hammer, everything looks like a nail.

Think about how you react when you feel somebody is pushing their product at you. The answer is almost always to push back or at least put up some barriers. That's a common response. Buyers put up barriers, they don't share information, they narrow access, and they don't trust what's being said to them.

The transaction becomes a dance, or perhaps a fight. Both sides probe for weaknesses, look for openings to attack or defend and ultimately beat the opponent. As a result, very few of these interactions lead to great, long-term relationships; instead, they reinforce the lack of trust and result in sub-optimal outcomes for both parties.

Becoming a trusted partner

The business opportunity here is to go beyond merely a successful sales relationship. The real potential is to become a trusted partner, sharing in the fruits of collaboration and synergy, creating value together. Here's how to use the three elements of the trust triangle to do just that.

Clarity

As the milkshake example illustrates, the first step towards creating clarity is to reverse your thinking about whatever it is you sell to your customers, whether it's a product or service. Stop thinking about what it does or trying to convince everybody you meet that it will be good for them. Instead, think about problems that potential customers may have either as consumers or businesses, and the results or benefits they might want to enjoy. If you can identify a group of individuals or businesses with a set of well-defined problems or results that align with the capabilities of your product or service, you have defined your market and you can take the analysis deeper.

Within that defined market, consider the specific problems or results that could be important; whether they're recognisable to the people in that market; and the potential value created by solving the problem or achieving the result. Use Table 6 to build your view of your market and create real clarity about the value you can create for the customer or client you want to serve.

This is a fundamental sales idea, and it's a critical part of the trust-building process because it grounds your actions and behaviours in the needs of the customer or client, not your need to sell. This is as much about what they do *not* need as what they do need; and being a high-trust salesperson depends on you being clear about this so that you can provide honest advice. Plus, of course, make sure you are targeting the right people.

TABLE 6. CLARITY ABOUT VALUE

What problems does your product or service solve? Or what results does it create? List them below	How would a customer or client see the problem or register the results? Be specific	What is the value to the customer or client of solving the problem or achieving the result?

Many businesses fail at this first hurdle. They fail to understand the market they should sell to and the value that they create for that market. This then transfers to a very poor, or perhaps generic, narrative which fails to maximise impact. The result is that they try to sell to the wrong people and trust is damaged.

A focus on clarity doesn't stop with the planning, however. As you choose trust and focus on building relationships, you need to refine your vision, maintaining the focus on creating and adding value to your customers or clients in a way that means they start to trust you. This creates value for you through their loyalty and willingness to pay you a reasonable rate for your goods and services.

Whether you are selling en masse to a consumer market, or in a highly bespoke way to high-value business clients, a focus on their needs, problems and desired results means that you have made the first step towards building trust. Business development needs to be a collaborative process, even for a mass market.

Find customers or clients that meet your analysis in Table 6 and share your proposals with them. Be ready to listen to their point of view rather than defending your own beliefs. The more open you can be to their experience and point of view, the more likely it is that you will get clarity about the value you might create for similar customers or clients, and the more knowledge you are building up of what makes sense to your customers or clients.

Don't underestimate the courage this takes. Having spent time working out why your product or service must be a winner, many people would rather not risk customers giving them negative feedback, so they avoid all feedback. When their product or service doesn't perform in the market as well as they would like, they can find plenty of excuses without being clear that the offer didn't resonate with the market in the first place.

Beyond value: shared ambition

Being willing to listen to your customers or clients and engaging them with testing value builds trust and a further opportunity to explore what they are trying to achieve in their world. Switching focus from you to them, from your success to theirs, makes you more trustworthy, and encourages broader and deeper discussions.

If both parties understand that their success needs to be aligned, and that they have the opportunity to create value together in a way they can't on their own, then it's a trust-based partnership with a shared ambition. Chapter 10 will look at the conversational skills that this requires, but it starts with the willingness to move from your solutions and to be deeply interested in the customers or clients, their business and their ambitions.

Character

Character – the behaviours of trust-based business development – is where the difference is made. Whatever you say about your desire to build trust, your customers or clients will judge you by your actions, and these flow from your beliefs. If you are driven by a transactional mindset, customers or clients will see that very quickly.

Your focus will be on closing the sale, persuading your customers or clients that your product or service is the right answer (whether you have investigated in depth what they are trying to achieve or not), and moving on to the next meeting, the next opportunity, the next customers or clients, whatever the outcome of the current discussion. Many people will tell you that sales is a numbers game. And they are right if you adopt a more traditional, transactional mindset.

Whatever you're selling, our evidence clearly shows that

you should focus on building a relationship. It's an approach that builds trust, increases win rates and, crucially, sales and customer satisfaction on both sides.

The buyer's decision process

Very few people are waiting to be sold to; impulse buying is rare, especially in a work context. People only start to feel a need for products and services when they need to solve a problem or achieve a specific result.

Therefore, if you are to build trust with customers or clients you must understand where they are in their decision-making journey and how you can support them along the way. Here's an outline of questions to ask during the decision-making process.

- Is there a problem or a result they want that is worthy of investment – and is it a priority?
- Can they solve the problem or achieve the result by themselves or do they need help?
- If they need help, who should help them?
- If you are the salesperson, is your solution the right one?

Understanding where a customer or client is in this process and being supportive of their journey – rather than trying to force the pace, push an agenda or product, and focus on your own interests – is about choosing trust. It dramatically changes the customer's perception of you and has an impact on their willingness to collaborate.

It leads you to share an understanding with the customers or clients about their priorities. It allows you to suggest innovations or provide input from your perspective that the customers or clients might find valuable. And, because it builds trust, it creates a strong competitive advantage where you can provide a solution to the problem or a way of achieving the desired result.

Having these kinds of business development conversations based on trust means that you need:

- a focus on the customer's priorities – rather than focusing on your need to meet your own goals
- an understanding of the customer's timescales and decision processes – rather than focusing on meeting your own targets
- interest in solving the customer's problems in the best possible way – not shoehorning your own capabilities into the picture where there are clearly better alternatives.

To many this approach will feel uncomfortable. It breaks so many of the norms of sales behaviour. But it clearly illustrates one of the benefits of building trust-based relationships as a means of business development: avoiding so much of the stress that "selling" creates. Because the customer or client isn't worried about your self-interest they are more open to your questions, your input and, in many cases, helping you to meet your needs as well. You can summarise this thought in a simple phrase: "Sell less, win more."

It's an approach that demonstrates all of the five principles of behaviour – and it works.

Consideration

The process set out above is all about consideration. It will determine the reaction you get from customers or clients. Consideration in this context has a very specific meaning: demonstrating by your words and your behaviour that you are interested in finding success for someone else, whether or not that ultimately means working with you or buying your products.

An important aspect of this consideration is to go beyond just the person you are talking to. Think about others who might be affected by their decision and consider their needs too. By thinking broadly about your customers or clients to show the broadest consideration for their success, you are far more likely to demonstrate trustworthiness and they will therefore be more prepared to be open with you.

Courage

A balance needs to be struck between demonstrating consideration and the need for your own business or organisation to achieve success too. If you have spent time gaining real clarity about where you can be successful and the value you bring to the market, your responsibility is to behave in a way that aligns with that vision. If what your customer or client defines as success aligns with your ambition, your behaviour will support that outcome. However, the true test of courage is how you behave when you conclude that what the customer or client wants does not align with your capabilities.

In this situation, it's critical that you both start with a common view of the outcomes required or you may be misjudging the potential for you to add value.

Next, you need to be ready to outline the gap you see between their needs and ambition and your capability. And you must have the courage to discuss with the customer or client what this gap implies. The outcomes of these discussions can be different and quite surprising.

- The customer or client understands the nature of the gap and you jointly agree that you shouldn't work together.
- The customer or client understands the gap and, because of the trust between you, engages you for a variant of the initial work or for part of the work.

- The customer or client identifies different areas of work on which they would like to collaborate.

Customers and clients value people who they trust and who they recognise are considerate of their needs and success. Many times, even if this discussion leads to no business being done, it still translates into success with that customer or client at a later stage because a relationship of trust has been created.

Honesty

Imagine you want to refurbish a house. You've solicited quotes from three builders. The first comes back with just an overall figure: no detail, simply a number. It is the lowest quote. The second sets out a detailed quote based on the specification.

The third provides a comparable (though higher) quote but also sets out many of the unknowns which could escalate the cost further, and suggests changes to the plans that would mitigate this. The builder provides a video shot at the premises pointing out in detail the areas where further investigation is needed, and makes suggestions about some of the details which would cost more but would be better solutions.

Which builder would you choose, whatever the cost comparison? In an area of significant investment, the last one stands out. It seems more likely you can trust that this builder was providing an honest assessment of both the job and the difficulties that might be faced. Their communication was open and honest, they demonstrated real expertise and provided real evidence of trustworthiness.

Everybody knows honesty when they see it or more clearly when they don't see it; linked to consistency, it will fundamentally affect whether you can build long-term relationships. Apart from pure commodity relationships (which shop you buy your baked beans from is not usually a relationship), most of us will go to a supplier who we believe to be honest about their goods, the service or the value for money. Even if they are less expensive, very few of us will want to have a relationship with a business or individual we know to be dishonest.

If you are to demonstrate the basis of a long-term relationship – consideration and courage – it goes hand in hand with honesty, both with yourself and with the customer or client. Many salespeople will recognise the nagging inner voice in discussions. It's that voice that's whispering things like: "I'm not sure you can really do this, but you have to win the deal!" or: "What they are asking for will never work but they want to buy! Let the delivery guys deal with it later."

Your inner voice may well be telling you to lie outright out of self-interest, or at best not be clear about the truth. However you cut it, it's simply not being honest and you know that nine times out of ten the customer or client comes to realise it pretty quickly.

Honesty with yourself about how you create value and your capability to do so is the foundation of trust. If you aren't honest with yourself, you'll struggle to be honest with others. Being honest with others is about being straightforward about the difficult as well as the easy. If you know the customer is mistaken, or you can't do something they need, or you have made a mistake, you need to say so in as clear way as you can, showing both consideration to them and the courage to do the right thing by yourself.

Loyalty

There are two types of loyalty in this context. One is to your customer or client: if you want to build loyal customers or clients, you need to demonstrate loyalty to them. The other is to your colleagues and supplier or partner: if you sell something they can't deliver, or at an unsustainable price, then you've damaged trust.

This can mean many things in different situations, but the principles set out in Chapter 4 will stand you in good stead. Here are some ideas. Also consider your own examples of how loyalty can be a key trust builder.

- Give credit where credit is due. If your role depends on the performance of key colleagues, make sure they get the recognition they deserve. You may be winning revenue, but you depend on them to deliver it.

- Follow the Golden Rule. Do unto others as you would have them do unto you. If you were in their shoes, would you buy whatever they are about to purchase? Do the right thing, even when you need the deal or when your commission is on the line.

- Don't bad-mouth your colleagues or customers to each other. Behave as if they are in the room even when they're not. The principle of emotional leakage means that people instinctively know how you feel about them even when you don't say it in front of them. This will affect how they feel about you.

- Think long term. If you want loyalty from your customer or client, and support from your colleagues, it starts with the way you demonstrate loyalty to them.

- It's often said that "loyalty is its own reward", and in business development it tangibly leads to better internal and external relationships as well.

Ambition

If there is one behaviour that people struggle with most, it's ambition. Not to be ambitious themselves, but in the ability to create a shared ambition, vision and narrative. Too many lack the consideration and courage to test with their customers or clients whether they understand the potential for synergy and are willing to invest to achieve its potential.

So what can you do that would be different? Start by sharing with your opposite number a belief in two things: the value of trust in relationships and the potential that working jointly could produce more than the sum of the parts. Remember the analogy of the planks shared earlier. One plank may well support 50 kg, but two together can support up to 500 kg.

Rather than worry about "selling" your service or product, starting with this discussion can change the whole way the relationship builds. Although not every customer or client will engage, you will be surprised at how many will, and those that do could easily turn into your best and longest relationships. That makes this discussion a valuable one with existing customers or clients as well as new ones.

Once this discussion has started you can apply the other behaviours of courage, consideration and loyalty to build powerful new visions for your partnership. These will naturally lead to commitments in terms of shared behaviours and capability in the form of a relationship agreement.

Business development meetings

In both business-to-business and business-to-consumer business development, you may well have meetings. These will vary from one-on-one and face-to-face meetings, to one-on-many or many-on-many, either face-to-face or virtual meetings. Whatever type of meetings they are, having a professional approach builds credibility and trust. What follows is a comprehensive checklist and a set of principles that you can add to your trust-based business development toolkit.

Before the meeting

Meetings are an important opportunity to "start as you mean to go on", demonstrating that you have the other party's success in mind, that you understand what they want to achieve and that you're prepared to support both.

Before you meet, we suggest the following activities to help make the meeting a success.

- Research the customer or client: individuals, company, sector, relationships, service history with your business.
- Call the customer or client and check who is attending and their purpose for being there.
- If people you haven't already spoken to will be at the meeting, try to call them for a short discussion in advance. Check out their perspective on why you are meeting.
- Agree an agenda to confirm the priority issues to be discussed, meeting outcomes and how the meeting will be run.
- Check logistics and make sure all the participants know where and when the meeting will take place, how to get there (or how to join a virtual meeting), and how long it is likely to last.
- Agree with your team how you will work together in the meeting to demonstrate your intent and achieve your agreed outcomes.
- Allocate roles including time manager, chairman and note-taker.
- Arrange a debrief session with your team.

Good preparation of this kind not only builds a base for trust, it also builds your confidence and sets up much more successful meetings.

During the meeting

- Check time and timing: how much time can the customer or client afford for this session? Stay aware of this and keep to the time allocated.

- Focus on the decision or outcome the customer or client has defined as success.

- Listen to understand, not simply to answer or get your point across.

- Meet any pushback by asking questions, focusing on understanding their point of view.

- Raise any issues that may get in the way of what the customer or client needs and try to resolve them to mutual satisfaction.

- Finish by testing progress against those outcomes.

- Agree next steps.

You'll notice that the checklist is focused on helping the customer or client meet their objectives. Most salespeople see a meeting as the opportunity to push whatever it is they are selling and in so doing create resistance. The alternative, focusing on the other party's success, builds trust and means the other party is more open to hearing how you might contribute. It sets the stage for the start of a partnership rather than a transaction.

Finishing the process of trust building means following up consistently.

After the meeting

- Summarise the discussion, capturing the key issues the customer or client shared with you, your input and suggestions and agreed next actions.

- Check that summary with them. Have you got it right? Have you left anything out?
- Modify the notes based on any feedback.
- Send them final, agreed notes.
- Share the output internally with all interested parties and save it so that you can refer to the notes before the next meeting.

These simple ideas will not only help you to build trust, but they will also save you time by ensuring that both you and your customers or clients are better prepared to move through the process to decide whether your product or service meets their needs. Too much time is wasted by salespeople who push the wrong product to the wrong people in the wrong way. And, as we've seen, the harder they push, the more resistance they create.

As you look through these suggested lists of activities, you may feel that you already do some or perhaps most of these things. If so, then you would agree with almost all the business development teams I have ever met. But very few do all or most of them *consistently*. If you want to be trustworthy, your business development behaviours need to be consistent, which brings us to the last of the three Cs of trust: capability.

Capability

What does it take to build great trust-based relationships as a business developer? Simple: the investment of time, money and people into the effort. Which, in capability terms, leads us to the concept of *relationship capital* – the sum of the time, money and people you can invest in any given relationship.

Like other forms of capital, relationship capital is in limited supply. You only have so much to go round. You can't afford to try to build deep, long-lasting trust-based relationships with everybody and expect to do a great job. This takes us back to two earlier ideas.

First, which markets, customers or clients have you identified where you are clear you can create value that they would recognise? Taken to the ultimate level, which are the potential customers or clients within those markets that are the best potential fit?

Second, how can you test and refine your offer with these potential customers or clients so that you are confident you have a good chance of a fit?

With this level of clarity, you can then start to plan your business, the mix of time, people and money (relationship capital) and how much you are going to invest in building each relationship. How many prospective relationships do you think you can develop? If the answer is thousands of relationships with only one business development person, you may be being overambitious. Our experience is that starting with a few and doing a really great job leads to greater learning and outcomes more quickly. You will need to assess your own market and routes to market to come up with your plan, and then execute and refine over time.

Investing relationship capital naturally continues once you have sold your product or service, as you manage the relationship you've established. Make sure that you and the customer or client discuss and agree the capabilities that you will both invest to achieve the agreed outcome, and how you will behave in the process. This discussion will naturally be a positive one, but take your courage in both hands to make sure you also discuss the big question of what to do if something goes wrong. This is the critical capability of governance explored above.

This book consistently demonstrates why choosing trust creates significant benefits on its own. In terms of business development, the difference is in the mindset that you bring to the table. Remember: 1 + 1 equals far more than 3. Belief in the power of mutual value and its ability to create better outcomes is at the core of trust-based selling and is the basis for all important relationships.

Applying the three Cs as outlined here will cement your success.

9

Building trust with suppliers

"Do not choose the one you don't trust
and trust the one you chose."

Ancient Chinese proverb

There were terrible floods in the English county of Cumbria in 2015. Farmers were tearing their hair out at the damage to crops and livestock. Members of the food industry which depended on them were equally worried.

The chief procurement officer of one of the country's biggest restaurant chains called one of its small farmer suppliers who had been affected. He asked how the supplier was and what difficulties he was facing. The answer surprised him.

"It's been terrible," came the reply. "I've lost much of my stock and produce. But don't worry, among all our customers I will make sure you get all your orders fulfilled."

"How can you promise that, and why are you doing so?" the procurement guy asked.

"Because of all our customers you are the only one to have called me to ask how I am and what is happening," came the reply. "So I will make sure we don't let you down."[1]

The way businesses manage those who supply them affects

every aspect of their operation, whatever the scale of the organisations involved. Because there is always choice, suppliers can decide who to please most when there are choices to be made. In a world of open communication, your customers will make decisions based on the whole process behind a product or service. Whether you are a corner shop depending on the local farmer and regular customers, or a major supermarket with a complex supply chain, the same principles apply.

The contrast is once again between being highly transactional – seeing suppliers as simply inputs that need to be managed and cost that needs to be minimised – or being trusted partners in the overall creation of value. The change in mindset leads to a change in behaviours.

Your suppliers will help determine whether you are trusted

The stakes are high. Everything your suppliers do or say about you, or how well they serve you, will reflect on your company, and how you treat them will help determine this. Smaller businesses will disproportionately benefit or suffer from this, as they rely hugely on fewer key suppliers, so if trust is damaged this could prove critical for them. Big organisations need to embed high-trust relationships in their supply chain as a matter of policy.

Patagonia is a multi-billion-dollar manufacturer and retailer of outdoor clothing and equipment. In 2022 its founder, Yvon Chouinard, created a purpose trust, into which he transferred all the company's voting stock. It meant that the company's values would be central to the business decisions made in the future, with the explicit purpose as being "in business to save our home planet". All the non-voting stock was transferred to a not-for-profit organisation dedicated to protecting the environment.[2]

This was the latest chapter in a company that has always

prided itself on demonstrating responsible business behaviours. Patagonia's approach to its supply chain is also driven by its purpose in what it calls its four-fold approach: it screens suppliers to meet sourcing, quality, social and environmental standards; if they fail any of these, they are not used. The company's supply chain strategy is driven by a series of measures, codes and affiliations to ethical bodies.[3]

The rewards for a successful supplier are high. The company's sales are in the billions. They claim to pay fair prices and the brand is now so trusted that being a Patagonia supplier is itself a quality standard respected by other customers.

As a result, Patagonia is one of the most trusted brands in the world. It is consistently rated as one of the most trusted companies in US research, a position that was consolidated by the transfer to a purpose trust. The company's view, according to its chairman, Charles Conn, is that "because we stand for something, we can also charge closer to what I would argue is the true economic cost of a garment".[4] In other words, the company can charge a premium to reflect the fact that it recognises real environmental and social costs, and customers trust its ethics and responsibility in everything it does.

Patagonia is an example of a company whose reputation is enhanced by the way it views its suppliers. Others demonstrate the opposite. In the 1990s, revelations about horrific sweatshop conditions damaged the reputation of footwear brand Nike, which denied all knowledge of the problem until it was forced to act. It's a reputational issue that has dogged the company ever since.[5]

In a landmark report, the International Trade Union Confederation showed how large companies rely on a huge supply chain workforce ("hidden workforces") to deliver their services.[6] So although they may demonstrate responsible leadership within their own organisation, they may be less responsible with the many people they are employing indirectly around the world.

For example, Walmart's 2.2 million-strong US workforce is dwarfed by the 10 million or so that ITUC claimed were employed by its suppliers at the time of the report. The figure for other retailers like the French firm Carrefour were, unsurprisingly, similar: Carrefour has 381,000 employees compared with a claimed 3.3 million employed by its suppliers.

Large industrial businesses were the same. In fact, the ITUC claims that 50 of the world's largest companies directly employ just 6% of the workforce which delivers their value. The remaining 94% are in their supply chains.

This is a function of the nature of increasingly global business and the complexity of what companies offer. But it also means that they depend on a wide range of other companies and their people to trade – and every one of these is a potential risk to their reputation, and therefore to the trust their customers and other stakeholders have in them.

The same is often true for smaller businesses. One of us ran a successful video production business. Although its sales and creative development was in-house, most of the production was carried out by freelance producers, camera crew and editors working at external production facilities. In the days before online distribution and viewing, hard copies (for the younger reader, these were called CDs, DVDs and even video cassettes) were produced by a specialist subcontractor.

It was crucial to the success of the firm that those representing it to clients in the field could be trusted, in terms of their professionalism and in the way they showed up. The firm was involved in news-related content, and so the production of the videos was time-critical, and, in many cases, favours were asked from the suppliers involved to meet urgent deadlines.

Without high levels of trust, many projects would have failed. Success was achieved by the quality of the relationships that had been built up. After every significant project, thank-you notes were written and calls were made; there were frequent social events organised to which all suppliers and contractors were invited; bills were paid on time; and there were frequent check-in discussions to make sure trust was maintained. At every opportunity, it was made clear to suppliers and partners that meeting the client needs was paramount – and that every effort would be made to help everyone support this culture.

Unfortunately, the way most supplier relationships have been historically managed has been transactional and cost-driven. A common transactional mindset seeks to protect the buyer and squeeze the price paid by the supplier. This is a power play which results in low trust, poor service and often a worse result for both buyer and seller. The seller seeks to recover margin through the life of a contract, a behaviour which drives even more defensive and transactional behaviour on the part of the former.

The truth is that, once a buying decision has been made, there is interdependence between the customer and the supplier. Behaving towards your suppliers in a power play backfires because it destroys what should be mutual interest in success.

If companies have extensive supply chains, often many times the size of their own business in terms of people and reach, each of these is a point of vulnerability for reputation or efficacy – and trust. The company's success depends on the effectiveness of this supply chain.

The wonder is that there are not more reputational disasters. What is certainly true is that there are many routine failures – cost overruns, service failures and delivery challenges. But even when this is not the case, outcomes are often less positive than they could be because the levels of collaboration are damaged through low trust.

Moving from transaction to trust

A high-trust buyer understands that their role is to manage these interconnected suppliers and partners. Even in the simplest of business situations, the different companies and people can be viewed as an ecosystem, not as a buyer and set of suppliers or a supply chain. This is a much more dynamic, interdependent view of the network involved in creating some kind of outcome.

It's a mindset as much as a strategy. It's a belief system that can change every interaction between a company and its suppliers, seeing them as long-term partners rather than one-off or short-term suppliers to be exploited.

Deloitte defines business ecosystems as "dynamic and co-evolving communities of diverse actors who create and capture new value through both collaboration and competition".[7] They all depend on each other to develop and maintain a healthy system, and to survive and thrive individually. Each one is in control of its own behaviours, actions and decisions, but each of these has an impact on others in the ecosystem – which in turn affects them too.

This fact alone makes building trust a key activity that someone in charge of suppliers can focus on to make the process as successful as possible in a sustainable way. Short-term success can be achieved through efficient transactions. Long-term success requires relationships between the people involved to have trust at their centres.

Instead of control, collaboration becomes the driving force within an ecosystem and this can lead to far greater collective innovation and higher performance for all those involved. But it requires deliberate and intentional design that can clash with existing cultural norms and approaches to risk. This is where the trust triangle can be a powerful foundation for a more effective supply chain.

As a way of shifting this mindset, it is worth using the term "supplier/partner" to describe those who provide services and goods to you or your company. The rest of this chapter will do this, except where the relationship is clearly transactional and the vendor is "merely" a supplier.

Clarity

Arm is an information technology hardware company founded with 12 engineers in a 14th-century barn in Cambridge in the UK in 1990. In July 2016 it was sold to Japan's SoftBank Group for $32bn. With sales of just $1.5bn, this was a high price – so why was it so valuable?

Its value derived from the way it managed its suppliers and partnerships, providing clarity about what it was trying to do, ambition about what could be achieved and a focus on collaboration as the way to innovate and grow. The company designs a specific type of microprocessor that requires fewer instructions, and therefore uses less power, than other chips. As a result, it became the industry standard in mobile devices and other fast-growing technologies. The critical skill that ARM developed was the ability to orchestrate the many different partners that made, developed and used its devices. With just 4,000 employees it dominated the hottest tech sectors because it created an ecosystem of global suppliers and partners who aligned with its vision and geared their capabilities towards it. This requires deep trust and a laser-focused clarity of purpose.[8]

An ecosystem requires leadership. The role of the leader here is to provide a clear vision, designed to align the actors in the ecosystem, and to ensure everyone understands what great looks like for the customer and the whole process. The foundation of this is trust, because the moment this is lost the whole thing can collapse like a pack of cards as partners and suppliers stop collaborating and the ecosystem begins to unravel.

Equally, there needs to be clarity about the relationship an organisation wants to develop with its suppliers and partners. Intentionally leading an effective ecosystem can be very different from running a tightly managed procurement-led, cost-driven supply chain. Too often, the way major procurement organisations define collaboration is: "You do as I say and you are being collaborative."

But a high-trust approach offers a strong sense of shared destiny, collective value creation and a desire that everyone in the ecosystem should benefit. The culture is one of collaboration, not conflict. To be truly intentional about this, it's important that the approach is stated explicitly in the clarity process as part of a relationship agreement. The capability process of the trust triangle means this will be fed through to governance as the relationships develop.

ARM was able to develop an ecosystem underpinned by the idea that "we get rich if our partners get rich". This is the mutual value mindset that underpins great supply chain ecosystems. Clarity of relationship, combined with clarity of ambition, is the foundation for higher levels of trust that will generate synergy, where everyone involved is adding to the collective value being created and feeding off the ideas, services and products of others in the system.

None of this removes the need for cost competitiveness, efficiency, performance, effectiveness and awareness of environmental, social and values issues. But these are more likely to be achieved and optimised by a collaborative, ecosystem approach. If everyone is aligned around some important ambitions, focused on clear outcomes and trusts in the relationship that underpins them, the outcomes will be easier to achieve. The ecosystem approach is inherently more flexible and agile, making it better at tackling problems and embracing opportunity.

Character

During the covid-19 pandemic, the way organisations treated their suppliers and partners was a clear indication of their true character, and one that will have had a long legacy for those who work with them. Their response indicated whether they could be trusted.

Morrisons is one of the UK's largest supermarket chains. Founded in 1899 on a market stall in Bradford, it has sought to retain a culture of being a place that helps everyone afford to eat well. Its roots in serving the northern English working classes remain evident. At the time of covid it was Britain's biggest single foodmaker, relying on a network of small and medium-sized food suppliers. These businesses were hit hard when the UK was locked down.

Morrisons responded by announcing it would pay these suppliers early to help with cashflow. It also reclassified smaller suppliers from those with £100,000 of business per year to those with £1m of business, bringing an additional 1,000 businesses into the scheme.

This mentality was part of an innovative, agile approach to the pandemic which saw Morrisons pioneer many new services while on what the chief executive David Potts called a "war footing", setting it up for sustained growth in the future.

I genuinely feel the company also played its full part in feeding the nation and it's properly been a company that's been there for all stakeholders. The Covid crisis has accelerated the new Morrisons as a truly distinctive business.[9]

Morrisons' approach to its suppliers and partners is part of a wider culture, demonstrating a business living its values not just with its own employees, customers and investors, but also with the people and organisations who provide it with the products it sells. Character is demonstrated by what you do. Morrisons demonstrated that its suppliers were not just disposable units of input, but genuine partners who are part of a bigger story.

Its actions also contrast with other big companies during the pandemic who simply announced to their suppliers that, because of their own cash flow issues, they would not pay anybody. This was perhaps understandable in difficult economic times, but the way that organisations dealt with this was an indicator of trust. They were storing up trouble for when the crisis was over.

The best organisations looked to communicate and collaborate, agreeing with their suppliers and partners what they could and should do to try to maintain their relationships and respective businesses.

Character is truly shown when there are difficulties. But it is demonstrated right from the start of the relationship in the intention you set out about how you want to engage. Choosing trust is the way to maximise the chance of collective, sustained success.

Capability

Remember that the two dimensions to capability are the way in which we manage and govern the relationship and how we combine our competencies. In an ecosystem approach to your suppliers and partners, these represent a fundamental change from traditional supply chain management.

The way the relationship is managed and governed

The first aspect of the capability dimension is the way relationships are managed and governed. If you have been a supplier to a large company or government buyer, the experience of dealing with procurement will almost certainly be all about the contract. The process of winning the business may have gone through a Request for Proposal process which will have been designed to minimise risk to the buyer, squeeze costs and pass as much of the liability for anything going wrong to the supplier. Boxes may have been ticked, a scorecard system may have been put in place, and both sides play a game to seek to achieve a successful outcome for themselves.

It is an utterly transactional process designed to depersonalise the decision, remove any value from an existing relationship and put the buyer in the driving seat. It demonstrates suspicion of the seller and an exercise of power by the buyer. Trust does not feature as a factor in this process, and so no one behaves in a trusting or trustworthy way. The goal for the supplier who enters this race is to win the business with as much margin left as they can achieve, while the buyer wants to pick a vendor who can credibly do the job as cost effectively as possible.

In many sectors procurement processes have moved on to some degree from this characterisation. Other factors are built in: looking at cultural issues, matching the way customers and suppliers work, putting quality controls in place. Environmental and social factors play a part too. But in so many situations the fundamental process of buying and selling in large organisations remains unchanged.

We have met many companies who describe this soul-destroying process. The outcomes are rarely the best for the buyer or seller. Often the wrong thing is being procured. Many vendors insist this is the case, but it is often difficult or impossible to provide this feedback before the buying decision has been made. The supplier, once it has won the gig, then often seeks to recover margin during the work through what are known as change notices. Since no one really knows what will happen when the work begins, any change to the original specification carries cost. This can be very profitable for the supplier because, having been appointed, it now has more power.

Importantly, collaboration between suppliers is not fundamental to this model. Vendors are hired in parallel with each other but are then expected to coordinate and collaborate. There is often nothing in the contractual process to ensure this will happen, and in many situations they are rivals for the customer's budget. The incentives to blame each other when things go wrong are high.

Combining competencies

The second aspect of capability determines whether trust can be achieved. It requires a transformation from a transactional purchase mindset to one where the outcome is a combination of competencies between the buyer and seller. It's not just about supplier or partner competency; the buyer also needs to have certain competencies for the seller to be able to do its job well. For example, if the buyer fails to make a timely decision, the seller may fail to provide them with what they need when they need it. If this happens consistently, this is not a mistake but an issue of competency on the part of the buyer. However, the buyer may claim that it is an issue of communication on the part of the seller. There are lots of reasons even in this simple situation where this can lead to blame or distrust.

In many cases, value is created by a combination of suppliers and partners providing some element of the overall value being created. Like ingredients in a cake, they provide much of what is needed and the buyer is the chef, combining these elements to produce the final product. Just by acknowledging this, the need for collaboration and trust becomes self-evident.

It's not that a classic efficient and process-driven supply chain doesn't work. Of course it does; businesses have adopted this approach successfully for many years. The problem is that it is rapidly becoming less fit for purpose in a fast-changing world, where innovation and flexibility are critical. As business academics Peter Williamson and Arnoud De Meyer say in their book *Ecosystem Edge*: "One of the most important advantages of an ecosystem approach is its ability to foster co-learning and catalyse innovation."[10]

This hinges on a strong sense of trusted partnership between those involved. The ambition should be to create behaviours which mean that those in the ecosystem will openly share ideas, respond quickly to events and work together to solve problems or approach opportunities. They trust each other. When things go wrong, they know that there is a sense of team even among different organisations providing inputs into the final product, all with a sense of collective value creation.

In a complex supply chain situation, one way to establish an ecosystem mentality is to develop a Relationship Agreement with all the parties involved. See them as ecosystem members, not just vendors. The core idea here is, as ever, to make trust central to the process of finding and choosing the right businesses with which to work. Critically, it must also then be central to the way you work together, with your relationships becoming a fundamental part of the delivery process. A Relationship Agreement, constantly reviewed and acted upon, will also mean that the quality of the way you work together will be included in the accountability and reward of everyone involved. The supply chain, becoming an ecosystem, can create a sense of teamwork.

Appointing new suppliers and partners

Here is a checklist to consider as you appoint suppliers or partners. Of course, they need to be competent and the business case for their costs must be solid. But assuming several fulfil these criteria, choose trust as a key way to decide who to work with and how to underpin the value you will create together.

At selection

Discussion and dialogue are critical if you are to have the best chance of selecting a trusted supplier or partner. How people interact will be critical to the work together and therefore feelings and reactions are as valuable as so-called "neutral" scoring criteria.

- Build into the selection process time to get to know each other, ideally tackling something together if possible.

   One way to do this is to find a pilot project that will both demonstrate value and provide valuable lessons for the main contract. Ideally pick something where the interdependencies can be seen and captured. For example, if you are appointing a consultancy to review some aspect of your business, see if there is a smaller part of the organisation where they can start. The idea is to identify how you work together as much as what they do.

- Discuss the relationship as part of the dialogue about the project. Think carefully in advance about how you want the relationship to be, not just the functional delivery.

  Consider scenarios where you will need to demonstrate trust as opposed to being contractual. For example, it is important to discuss how you will both be expected to behave if something goes wrong. Having an open and honest dialogue about this will show both of you whether you will work well together. If you draft a relationship agreement, capture the conclusions of this discussion.

- If feasible, ask potential suppliers and partners to work alongside each other in a workshop or project scoping exercise. Look out for collaborative behaviours. Ask yourself, when you see them in action, whom you trust most.

  This is becoming common in many construction projects, where collaboration is key. One of the challenges here is to ensure that the people who engage in the process are also those who will work on the project. Making sure this is the case should be part of the engagement criteria.

  We worked on a project with a supplier where the team working on a project was entirely different from the one that had won it. The result was that none of them had any idea about the behaviours that had been demonstrated or promised at the time of winning the bid – they were working to the contract. It was going badly, and when we showed them what had been originally promised, and the output from our interviews with those originally involved, they realised the problem and were able to resolve it.

- Identify the values and purpose of the supplier or partner and check whether these align with your own. If these are not in evidence, that in itself tells you something. Be clear about what matters to you and ensure this is true for the other parties too.

Identifying values is much more than confirming that they have the right words on their website. Find evidence that they put them into practice. Gather stories and testimonials that they live these values.

Then do something even more difficult. Ask yourself: does your organisation live its values? This is a powerful question. Look for evidence that you have a set of principles beyond cost control. This is all about what will work in the real world when you are meant to be collaborating. This exercise could prove to be a valuable way to ensure you are a high-trust buyer.

- Consider the value that is created by existing relationships and the degree to which trust already exists and has been earned. Having partners who work well with your organisation (and together) is in itself part of what they bring to you. Build this into the buying decision.

Smaller organisations instinctively understand this. Where they have worked together with a supplier or partner, that relationship will determine future orders. But bigger ones often struggle under the weight of procurement procedures which focus on price-driven competitive quotes. Relationships will help the work together succeed; if these exist, they should be recognised and valued.

- Put in place relationship governance processes in line with the capability dimension and ensure those involved agree them as part of any negotiations.

Chapter 5 set out ways to make relationship governance part of your work together, whatever the scale of the enterprise or project. The informal and formal processes outlined there are designed to provide a solid foundation for relationships. It is important to track this as much as the practical delivery when you start to work together.

Working together

Regularly review the relationship in line with agreed governance processes. This should be separate from any continuing technical reviews.

As part of this review process, continually check in with your own team and your suppliers and partners. Ask the question openly: do you trust each other? Identifying any behaviours that damage trust will make mutual success more likely.

- Identify specific situations where trust has been under stress.

  You can simply discuss together how these can be handled better in future. In more complex situations, structure this into a workshop. Capture what you decide in a way that is shared and agreed.

- Include accountabilities.

  These must be mutual – it is not just about the supplier or partner demonstrating what you consider to be trustworthy behaviours. They can equally call you out for actions or decisions that can damage trust, and part of the behaviour of openness is to welcome this as part of the development of mutual trust.

- Publicly celebrate examples of great relationship behaviours.

  Examples of great collaboration, mutual problem-solving and trusting actions are wonderful ways to encourage more of the same. Often companies celebrate and communicate what their own people do, but not what is done by their suppliers or partners. If they are part of your ecosystem, they are on the team. Treat them as such.

- Make it clear that such stories are rewarded and form part of the award of future business.

There should be openly commercial benefits for high-trust relationship building. The opposite can also be true – where consistently poor relationship behaviour is communicated and forms part of the overall assessment of the work.

You are all part of the same team

Every supplier or partner situation is different. This chapter lays out some important principles that can turn a transactional set of commercial arrangements into a truly collaborative ecosystem of suppliers and partners who trust each other. The benefits of this are enormous, especially where the parties have to work together in a complex way to achieve an overall outcome, or there is likely to be change and the need for agility and adaptation, and where the intention is to have long-term, consistent relationships.

Suppliers and partners are effectively an extension of your core business. That's why developing a highly collaborative culture, with a strong sense of shared destiny, will create far greater overall value. A customer trusts a vendor if they feel the vendor has their interests at heart. Similarly, a supplier or partner who knows the buyer cares that they are treated fairly and that they benefit from the relationship. They will give discretionary effort and do everything they can to help the buyer achieve success.

This requires a mindset shift from supply chain to ecosystem, a move from seeing supplies or partners as external vendors to seeing them as people who are on the team. It requires everyone to choose trust.

10

Conversations that build trust

"A conversation is a dialogue, not a monologue."

Truman Capote, American novelist

A colleague was preparing for an important meeting with a potential client. Apart from a short conversation on the phone to arrange the meeting and set an agenda, they hadn't met and didn't know each other personally. My colleague had done his research and was in the middle of putting together what he hoped would be an impressive PowerPoint presentation to demonstrate his expertise. I was worried about whether this was really the best approach.

I asked him to stop a minute and answer a short question. "When you went on the first date with your partner, what did you do?" And he told me. "We went to a nice restaurant. I asked her a couple of questions and then I listened to her tell me a lot about herself. She really opened up and it turned out we had a lot of things in common."

I couldn't resist asking him: "Did you have a presentation about how good a potential partner you were? Did you offer her some references about your expertise?"

Of course, the answer was no, because he knew that

conversation, and especially listening, is a powerful way of choosing trust and building strong relationships. And it's as true in business as in our personal life.

Ultimately, trust between people is built on interactions – the conversations and meetings that define who and what we are in the eyes of others. This chapter explores how you can craft these interactions in a way that will positively support your intention to choose trust. It shows how to translate the three elements of the trust triangle into the language and conversations that will help you to build trusted relationships at work.

People will assess your trustworthiness based on how you behave as much as what you say. So it helps to use a style of conversation that demonstrates your intent to be trustworthy and helps to build trust with others.

Figure 7 on the next page shows a simple flow for a high-trust conversation, which may take place over several meetings or calls. It's important to complete each stage before moving on to the next. You may not need or choose to use each stage in every conversation, but the general flow of a high-trust conversation is to explore, to broaden the discussion, to focus on what really matters and what to do about it. It starts with how you approach the conversation in the first place.

Your approach to the conversation

Whether the conversation is casual or formal, you can use the simple acronym OIL to be intentionally high trust. OIL stands for:

· Open to emotion
· Intend to help
· Listen to understand.

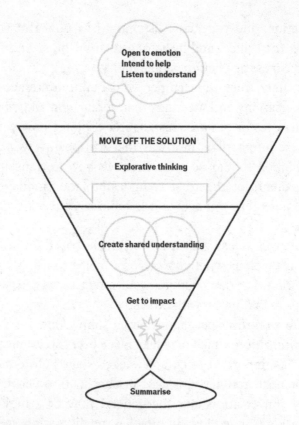

Figure 7: **High-trust conversations**

Open to emotion

Many people veer away from responding to emotions; after all, this is "about business". But that's a serious mistake.

If the person you are talking to is energised by the topic – they could be excited or stressed, motivated or challenged by the situation they find themselves in – your willingness to recognise and acknowledge that fact in a conversation can dramatically change the whole tenor of the discussion, as well as the recognition of your intent by the other party.

Brene Brown put the idea very simply in her book *Dare to Lead* when she wrote:

> Empathy is a choice. And it's a vulnerable choice, because if I were to choose to connect with you through empathy, I would have to connect with something in myself that knows that feeling. In the face of a difficult conversation, [...] it's our instinct as human beings to try to make things better. We want to fix, we want to give advice. But empathy isn't about fixing, it's the brave choice to be with someone in their darkness – not to race to turn on the light so we feel better.[1]

So the difference is to hear the words and read and respond to the emotion. To do this we simply say something which refers to the emotional content we have heard and/or observed, such as:

- You seem excited about ...
- What you've described sounds stressful.
- This sounds like something you are very motivated to achieve.
- I get the feeling this is very challenging for you and the business.

This is a powerful way to engage at a human level and to build on your intent to be open and trustworthy. We are actually all acutely attuned to read the messages that others give off. It is the ability to read these messages and to respond through empathy that can make all the difference to the quality of the conversation and the trust we create. Emotions are as important as the facts.

The best way to understand how empathy works, and our ability to read and respond to emotions, is to practise. Try the exercise on the following page.

Exercise: Practising empathy

Find somebody to work with on this and explain that you want to practise being more empathic.

Ask them to share something with you that they are excited or worried about. Don't try to solve the problem or give them the answer. Listen hard to understand and then simply repeat what you heard, including the emotion that you heard or sensed. Use phrases such as:

"You seem excited about ..."

"I sense you are worried about ..."

"It feels like you are concerned about ..."

Keep your response short and don't ask any further questions about the point they have just raised. Let your colleague respond and, once again, listen to understand the response and the emotion before replying again.

When you have tried this for a couple of minutes, ask your colleague for some feedback.

- Did they feel your intent to listen?
- Did they feel more understood?
- What did they get from this conversation?

Intend to help

The way you talk to others says a lot about your intent to build trust.

To build trust, the other party in the conversation needs to understand that you are deeply interested in them, their beliefs and views, and your intention is that this conversation should be successful or valuable for them. This is the behaviour of consideration in action. The opposite of consideration may be perceived as self-interest, that you are primarily interested in a conversation for what's in it for you, that you win the argument or make your point heard first. Anything you do that smacks of self-interest as your primary driver in a conversation risks shutting the other party down and reducing your opportunity to build trust.

Getting shared understanding of value in a conversation and starting with the other party's success is a significant change for many of us. Two of my friends, who describe themselves as neuro-untypical, taught me a great lesson. They realised that many of their conversations ended up either in disagreements or aggravation because one party or the other didn't understand what the conversation was trying to achieve.

They developed a simple check-in on the lines of: "Is this conversation a rant so you can blow off steam, or are you looking for my help and advice?" When they both knew what they were looking for from the conversation they could engage productively, and their relationship became more rewarding. This is a lesson you can apply in any conversation, at work as well as in life.

The principle of clarity applies here too. Are you simply trying to serve your own ends or are you both clear what the conversation is trying to achieve? If you are trying to build trust, being open to the needs of the other party first, and being prepared to listen, will greatly enhance your relationship.

It's worth thinking about how you can make sure people understand your intent in conversations. One way of doing this is to be explicit about it with the other party, as long as your behaviour aligns with that intent. Too often salespeople say they are there to help their customer and then spend the next half of the conversation explaining what they do rather than exploring what the other person needs. In this situation, self-interest is so evident that the customer quickly shuts down.

Listen to understand

Your high-trust intention (or the opposite) will also come out in the way you listen. The next time you are having an important conversation with somebody, focus on your listening and ask yourself: what's the purpose of my listening?

You might be listening for a number of reasons.

- To respond or answer. You might be trying to understand the question so that you can give your best answer. Using clarification questions will help you give the best possible answers.

- To get your opportunity to speak. If you feel you are right or have the best answer, you may stop listening to the other person and simply be waiting for a break in the conversation so you can get your own ideas over.

- To understand. Demonstrate by your attitude and your open questions that you really want to understand. Use summarising as a way of confirming understanding. Use empathy to respond to feelings as well as content.

When you can honestly say your focus is on the last of these reasons, listening to understand not just the facts but also how the other person is feeling, your intent to build trust will be clear to the other party.

Conversations that create value

People are in conversation for much of the day. This book focuses on key conversations you may have at work that create value, however value is defined, whether value is monetary or not, conversations with colleagues or clients that lead to decisions, and how you participate in those conversations to build trust and relationships. Without a deliberate process for conversations that build trust, people tend to rely on their natural ability, which is at best variable. It may also let you down when the information is important to the other party, and you are internally focused on thinking of the next critical question rather than doing what you should be doing – listening.

Let's take an example. You are in a team and a member of the team comes to a meeting and makes a proposal – something that's going to take time and resources. Think about when you have been around that table in that kind of situation. What tends to get discussed first is whether the proposal will work, and possibly refining the proposal to "make it work". Then the conversation quickly turns to how, when and who.

What we fail to understand is what is driving the desire for action or change. What is your colleague or client seeing that caused them to make their proposal? This is their "why", and ignoring the "why" fails to create real clarity about the ambition, or the problem the proposer was trying to solve, or the result they were trying to achieve.

Imagine a senior leader who declares: "We need to change the marketing approach!" Cue much discussion and activity, but no one thinks to ask critical questions to help them to understand how the leader arrived at the idea – which, in the end, could lead to some expensive mistakes. Similarly, you may be asked by customers to talk about how you could do something, or to quote for supplying goods or services, and yet fail to explore the "why".

There's a good reason for this: people love to spring into action and focus on solutions rather than causes because they have learned to be transactional and convergent in their thinking. The alternative is to use explorative thinking (moving away from the suggestion or solution) to build a shared understanding of the why, to build a shared ambition, and then to converge on an agreed way forward.

Explorative thinking establishes clarity

The first step in the explorative thought process is to move off the solution, whether that's come from a question or request by somebody we are talking to, or even something we would like to propose. This may seem counter-intuitive, but it's a classic case of "go slow to speed up". So how do you do this?

First, let's recognise a solution when it appears. Solution requests or suggestions take many forms both in internal discussions and with customers and clients. They are often associated with some form of proposed change. "Solution request" questions can be prefaced by phrases such as:

· What we need is ...
· What we should do is ...
· Here's a suggestion ...
· Do you have any ideas about ...
· What would be your approach to ...

Let's imagine a scenario. In a sales situation, your customer suggests they need your product or service and asks for a proposal. Instead of jumping in and starting to specify exactly what you should sell them, take a moment and ask one of the following "move off the solution" questions instead.

· What problems might you hope this will solve?

Or:

· What results are you hoping this solution might achieve?

Only when you have a sense of the problems or results as the customer sees them can you start to delve deeper to really understand how they see the situation.

A key word of caution here on language. Remember the

story in Chapter 4 of the divorcing couple who didn't seem to communicate. The common use of language doesn't necessarily imply common meaning. Explorative thinking also means challenging assumptions about shared meaning to make sure that everyone involved has the same understanding of language and intent.

Exercise: Explorative thinking

Make a list of all the products or solutions that your client may buy from you. Give the list to a partner or colleague and get them to ask you a "solution request" question.

For example:

"We're interested in …. Can you tell us how it might work?"

Or simply:

"Can you give me a quote for …?"

For each product or service on your list, practise using a "move off the solution" question. For example:

"What problems were you hoping to solve by buying …?"

"What results are you hoping this solution might achieve?"

As necessary, clarify any terms using the phrase:

"When you say …, what do you mean by that?"

Keep practising until you are confident you can use this approach habitually.

Creating shared understanding

Having moved off the solution, the path to mutual understanding is to follow the evidence. Helping your partner or colleague to confirm the value you're trying to create together – or the cost you're trying to reduce – is a powerful way to ensure clarity and therefore the basis for trust.

Many times the language you use can be a high-level

abstraction or description, open to misunderstanding, misinterpretation or confusion. Your ambition should be to move through these high-level abstractions to detailed and shared understanding. It's like peeling an onion – and this gives the best clue as to how you can approach any issue that requires analysis or deeper shared understanding. Think of what you first hear as the outer skin of the onion. You can explore the details by asking evidence questions.

Evidence questions start with "How", "What", "Where", "Which", "When" and "Who". For example, you could ask any of the following questions.

- How has this occurred?
- What tells us this is an issue?
- Where is the issue affecting us?
- Which parts of the business are affected?
- When did this happen?
- Who is most affected by this issue?

These kinds of questions allow your partner or colleague to share an understanding of the outer layer before peeling that back with a question based on a summary of what you just learned and adding: "And if that happens, then what happens next?"

This process of evidence questioning should be repeated until both parties have a deep and shared understanding. It builds trust because you demonstrate your intent to understand the other party. It also helps them to think clearly and perhaps more deeply about what they are trying to achieve, and even whether it's needed or valuable.

Getting to value

Good decision-making, shared commitment and creating value together often revolve around getting agreement on the value – of the decision you make, the product or service you supply or the value of the problem or result you are describing. If you are to build trusted relationships, working towards a shared ambition that has a specific value – a value that you have jointly agreed – helps with three things.

1. To make the commitments in terms of resources needed to achieve an agreed outcome.
2. To keep committed over a period of time, stopping the risk of chasing the "new and shiny" opportunity or suggestion.
3. As results arrive, it reminds you of the value you set out to achieve, and the contribution that a collaborative relationship has created.

As you think about decisions you have been involved in, or services or products you have sold, ask yourself how often you had a conversation with the other party about the value they were hoping to create. Based on our interaction with thousands of business people, if you are honest, the answer will be very seldom.

One of the possible issues here is worrying that, if the impact is measured in monetary terms, the discussion could be especially difficult. You might be concerned that you might disturb a relationship, perhaps upset your opposite number by questioning their sense of the value or numbers. Or perhaps it might be something you feel they won't trust you with. Either way, when you fall into this transactional thinking and don't work to get a shared understanding of the impact, you fail to apply either the consideration or the courage needed to build a deep trust-based relationship.

Once you move away from solutions and start peeling away the layers of the onion to move towards value, you need to apply a final simple process to understand that value in a way that both parties recognise.

When peeling the onion, at some point your opposite number may mention something which has a measurable value. It's at this point that you should ask the following questions.

- Is that something you measure?
- How do you measure it?
- What's the number currently?
- If you succeeded, what would that number be?
- What would be the value to you or the business of achieving that change?

Bear in mind that not everything needs to have a financial impact. You may have agreed an important value which may be measurable but not necessarily financial. Examples might include customer satisfaction, employee engagement, or even levels of trust. What's important is that you have a shared understanding of the value that you are both trying to achieve.

Here's a worked example where the output might be financial. A colleague wants to reduce failure on a production line.

Is failure rate something we measure?	Yes
How do you measure it?	Failures per thousand
What's the current failure rate?	0.25
If you applied the change you are thinking of, what would that number be?	0.125
What would be the value to the business of achieving that change?	

The final question may require significant thought or analysis to translate this change to monetary value but it's important that this final step is not shirked. Although it's true that many decisions are made on emotion backed up by data, this approach is vital for building clarity and commitment.

Keep the ideas of consideration and courage equally in mind throughout these discussions. As you listen to the answers continue to use the skills outlined earlier to clarify and confirm understanding.

Summarising as a trust builder

When you are listening to understand and asking great questions, summarise the discussion on a regular basis. This shows that you are listening in such a way that you can repeat what you have heard. When you summarise, simply reflect what you heard, without comment or interpretation, to demonstrate the value you place on what the other person is saying. This conveys consideration and a focus on the other party. In doing so you encourage the other party to be open with you and establish trust.

The language of trust

Consideration and courage lead to a different vocabulary, which reflects collaboration and mutual interest over and above personal needs. It's important to recognise the difference and thoughtfully apply language that reflects your intention to build trust.

Look at the examples on the following page and notice the difference.

Transactional or self-interested language	Mutual exploration
What I need to understand is ...	It would be helpful to establish a shared understanding about ...
My objective for this meeting is ...	By the end of the meeting it would be great if we could ...
I want to convince you that ...	I want us to decide whether ...
I know what we need to do ...	I'd like to explore your thoughts on an idea ...
This project is on track, on time and on budget	Let's share with you our current progress and agree whether we are happy with the status of the project
I'm sure ...	Let me share my thinking and get your view
I have a plan for the next steps I'd like to get your buy-in	It would be good to get your views on whether this plan would work
Here's what I want you to do, and I'm holding you accountable	If we are agreed on what you are going to do, how would you propose reporting on progress?

Without meaning to, much of the language you hear will emphasise the needs of the speaker, not the person they are talking to. The emphasis tends to be on what they need in any particular situation, or their need to prove themselves right. In contrast, the language of trust emphasises mutual agreement, collaboration, shared outcomes and openness to input from the other party. It flows naturally from a belief that two or more people collaborating will typically outperform an individual certain of their own convictions.

Exercise: Planning an exchange

Think about an upcoming meeting.

- What do you want the meeting to decide?

- How will you express this to gain agreement based on shared understanding?
- Write down and practise how you will share this in the meeting.

Bringing it all together

Here's a simple example of how to apply the process outlined in Figure 5. In this example, team member A has suggested that her organisation should invest in a new customer relationship management (CRM) system.

You: This sounds interesting. What problems made you feel we should invest in a new CRM? *[Move off the solution]*

A: We simply aren't tracking our opportunities properly.

You: It would be helpful to understand how this shows up. *[Peel the onion – Evidence]*

A: I have to keep chasing the sales team to tell me what they are doing.

You: And if you aren't tracking opportunities properly, then what happens? *[Peel the onion – Impact question]*

A: We aren't putting the right effort into the right opportunities.

You: When did this start to be a problem? *[Peel the onion – Evidence]*

A: It became really important last quarter when we began to miss our targets.

You: So if you aren't putting the right effort into the right opportunities, then what happens? *[Peel the onion – Impact]*

A: Our win rate is too low.

You: Is win rate something you measure? *[Impact]*

A: Yes, of course.

You: How do you measure it?

A: We look at it quarter by quarter.

You: What's the current win rate?

A: One in eight.

You: If we implemented a new system, what would the win rate be?

A: If we could track our opportunities, I think we could get that up to one in six.

You: What would be the value to you or the business of achieving that change?

A: If we succeed, that would create a £3m upside to the business.

You: Let me see if I have heard this correctly. You want to invest in a new CRM system that would allow you to track opportunities and put your best efforts into the right ones. You think that because you can't do that today your win rate is down at one in eight but that with the new CRM you could get that up to one in six, resulting in an additional £3m to the business. Did I get that right? *[Summary]*

Towards resolution or outcome

So far, this process has stayed with explorative thinking; you have understood, but neither agreed nor disagreed. You have opened up the discussion to explore how the other party has reached their view.

There are several possibilities for how this kind of conversation can move on.

1. You understand and agree that the problem needs resolving.
2. You understand but don't agree with the conclusion or solution that the other party has reached.
3. You don't understand.

1. You understand and agree that the problem needs resolving

You can now switch to convergent rather than explorative thinking, focusing on a solution or agreed action. You can explore in more depth the solution the other party has suggested and support their thinking around implementing it.

The outcome is clarity about what the two parties are trying to achieve, and a commitment to why it needs to happen.

2. You understand but don't agree with the conclusion or solution that the other party has reached

It's important to stay with the relationship, but not to agree until you fully share the rationale. You will need to continue to explore how and why the other party reached their conclusion. Useful language at this point can include questions such as:

- Can you help me understand what led you to that idea?
- What specifically makes you believe that ...?
- What happens after this?

Keep summarising what you hear to give the other party the opportunity to clarify your understanding, or add to it with new ideas or input.

Although you may not reach agreement through this exploration, you will be clear about each other's view. This in itself is valuable and you can reach a shared decision about next steps.

3. You don't understand

Where you need to get clear evidence and impact that you can understand, you need to flag this to the other person rather than fall into argument. Remember that you are challenging a belief or an idea that the other party may feel strongly about, so stay considerate to their needs. But this must be balanced with the courage to stay true to your own beliefs. One way of doing this is to restate what you are hearing and invite the other party to explore the issue with you.

Summarising what you have heard might be something along these lines:

> "I recognise that you feel this makes sense and is clear,
> but I'm struggling to understand how this ties together,
> particularly in the area of ... What am I missing?"

By giving the other party the opportunity to understand the specifics of your concern, they can either share more information, or they can acknowledge the gap and together you can establish whether there is a course of action which may bridge the gap.

*

One of the interesting things that can come out of these kind of discussions is that both parties can acknowledge when new ideas have come to light. Whereas transactional conversations are often about winning the argument or convincing somebody else you are right, true trust-based discussions create an environment where both parties are willing to learn from each other, to admit when new information has changed their view, and to build on each other's ideas. In these conversations, once one party has deeply understood the other's point of view, evidence and impact, they are free to share their own thinking, with both parties willing to adopt, modify or discard ideas that don't move them forward.

Collaborative discussion can be uncomfortable. People will challenge each other, offer alternatives and disagree. However, if they do so in the spirit of honesty, loyalty and the ambition to create a better outcome, the result is more likely to succeed because it flows from clarity and shared commitment. Practising your conversational and listening skills will create better interaction, teamwork, trust and relationships in every walk of life.

Epilogue
Trust is a choice

"To know and not do, is not to know."

Goethe, German writer and statesman

There are a lot of stories and anecdotes in this book that show how people have destroyed trust through their actions and behaviours. None of them set out to do so. No leader says: "I will do something that means no one will trust me again." No salesperson sets out to damage the trust their customer has in them or their company. No colleague goes to work to damage any trust others have in them or to work with others they don't trust.

Yet it happens every day, in every context. When it comes to trust, you deposit in pence and withdraw in pounds. Trust is hard to create and easy to destroy and, in a world where distrust is much more prevalent than before, this is truer than ever.

People act according to what they believe is the right thing to do at that moment, often based on practical or technical reasons and under pressure. Maybe they feel they are being "professional" or maybe they have lived in a transactional world for so long they aren't stopping to think. The question of trust is not at the front of their mind. By not choosing trust, they inadvertently choose mistrust. This book has highlighted some of the consequences of this. You can surely think of many others.

If you are not behaving consciously, you are doing so unconsciously, and that leads to assumptions, actions and consequences that you may never have intended or even considered. That's why trust is a conscious choice, deliberately designed into relationships as an intentional focus, so that when things happen that no one could foresee, there is a bond between those involved that helps them tackle issues together.

It's worth repeating why this is so important. Everyone has choice about what they do, how they react and what decisions they make. Those who are trustworthy are chosen more often, those who trust and feel trusted perform better, those who work in a high-trust environment thrive.

But the exact opposite is also true. And the pressure to be transactional in every interaction can be remorseless. That's why it makes sense to be the person who stands out by focusing on being a trusted human. People want to trust and be trusted, and in a world where this is in short supply, those who decide that this is where they stand will be more attractive to customers, employers, colleagues and partners.

Every working relationship you have can be considered through this lens. The work you need to do together – the technical, financial, operational and delivery issues – may be where many people put most of their focus. But in parallel to this is the relationship you have. This involves emotions, perceptions and judgements. Personalities come into play, both for the individuals and their organisations or teams. This will determine the success of work you do together just as much, but will get a fraction of the attention.

That is what this book has set out to put right. It is intended as a guide that provides a structure for consciously choosing trust, but even if you have found just one or two ideas at any stage of the process that you can use in your day-to-day work, then it has achieved its ambition.

Our focus is on people at work. Our belief is that this philosophy is sorely lacking in so many contexts, and we hope that changing people's mindset and behaviours in one area may also see a benefit in all aspects of their life. That is our wish for you.

Acknowledgements

Stuart Maister

Everything I have ever done professionally has been based on my original training as a TV and radio reporter. A broadcast journalist needs to get to the heart of a story rapidly, translate complexity in a simple way geared towards the audience they serve, and then communicate it clearly. My contribution to the thinking and writing in this book derives from the insights gained over decades of applying those skills with leaders from all types of business. It is always clear to me they know too much, and are so immersed in the need to get things done that simple truths often get lost.

So I am grateful to all the people at the BBC and elsewhere who trained me to be a journalist, and to the many clients with whom I have worked over decades who have been kind enough to let me help them gain clarity and communicate it effectively.

Kevin Vaughan-Smith

If you have ever tried to explain to your children what you do, you may have shared my experience. What seems simple when you are deeply involved becomes difficult to explain to anybody who isn't. Having to think hard about what I believe, and over the years explain it to my children and answer their questions, led me to question myself in a way that inspired much of what I have contributed to our book. My thanks to them and to my wife

Hayley for her tireless input and review. And finally, thanks to our clients who have engaged with us so freely, and tested and applied our ideas so enthusiastically.

Notes

Chapter 1. The power of trust – and why most people don't choose it

1. K. Brown and I.J. Dugan, "Arthur Andersen's fall from grace is a sad tale of greed and miscues", *Wall Street Journal* (June 7th 2002). A great summary of how cultural change led to this downfall.
2. "How the Big Bang changed the City of London for ever", BBC News (October 27th 2016). This is a very good summary of the Big Bang and its impact.
3. S.M.R. Covey with R.R. Merrill, *The Speed of Trust* (Simon & Schuster, 2008).
4. Interview with Stuart Maister in the podcast 'Choose Trust', acast.com (March 2023).
5. Britannica has a very good explanation of confirmation bias: britannica.com
6. Developed from the concept of a paradigm shift as explained in S.R. Covey, *The 7 Habits of Highly Effective People* (Simon & Schuster, 1989).

Chapter 2. Choose trust to create more value

1. Studies that are worthy of review include: "Improving employee engagement to drive retention and performance", LumApps (2023); and P.J. Zak, "The neuroscience of trust", *Harvard Business Review* (Jan–Feb 2017).

2. A.C. Edmondson, *The Fearless Organization: Creating Psychological Safety in the Workplace for Learning, Innovation, and Growth* (Wiley, 2019).

3. "How trust in your organization can drive performance", Deloitte. deloitte.com/global/en/issues/trust.html

4. First featured in the book *The Trusted Advisor* by D.H. Maister, C.H. Green and R.M. Galford (Simon & Schuster, 2000).

5. Figure X from *The Trusted Advisor* by D.H. Maister, C.H. Green and R.M. Galford (Simon & Schuster, 2002). Copyright © David Maister, Charles Green and Robert Galford 2002. Reprinted by kind permission from David Maister, Charles Green and Robert Galford.

6. R. Semler, *The Seven-Day Weekend: A Better Way to Work in the 21st Century* (Random House, 2003).

Chapter 3. Clarity: the foundation of trust

1. "Communication barriers in the modern workplace", The Economist Intelligence Unit (2018).

2. "Mars Climate Orbiter Mishap Investigation Board Phase I Report", NASA (November 10th 1999).

3. Interview with authors on the 'Choose Trust' podcast, February 2023. shows.acast.com/choose-trust/episodes/transforming-relationships-in-an-industry-where-conflict-was

4. M. Kapko, "Apple and IBM partnership yields 100 iOS enterprise apps", CIO (December 18th 2015).

Chapter 4. Character: the behaviours that build trust

1. "2024 Edelman Trust Barometer: Global Report", Edelman (2024).

2. The story of overspend in the HS2 project is outlined

in this report: "High Speed Two: Euston", National Audit Office (March 24th 2023). nao.org.uk/wp-content/uploads/2023/03/high-speed-two-euston.pdf

3. A full description of the Texas childcare system debacle is given here: "Case study 14: how Texas wasted $367 million on an unusable child support enforcement system", Henrico Dolfing (October 24th 2020).

4. J. Collins, *Good to Great: Why Some Companies Make the Leap ... and Others Don't* (Random House, 2001).

5. This quote is often attributed to the great industrialist Henry Ford (among others).

Chapter 5. Capability: the ability to work together

1. Podcast interview by the authors with Gregor Craig, June 2023. "Inside the mind of a construction sector leader", Choose Trust episode 6, Acast (June 14th 2023).

Chapter 6. Being a high-trust leader

1. C. Feser, F. Mayol and R. Srinivasan, "Decoding leadership: what really matters", *McKinsey Quarterly* (January 1st 2015).

2. J. Smythe, *The CEO: Chief Engagement Officer. Turning Hierarchy Upside Down to Drive Performance* (Gower, 2012).

3. S. Western, *Leadership: A Critical Text*, 3rd edn (Sage, 2019).

4. A great summary of the Travis Kalanick/Uber story can be found in: M. Isaac, "'I'm a terrible person': behind the epic meltdown that ended Travis Kalanick", *Vanity Fair* (September 3rd 2019).

5. The New Management Initiative at Samsung was summarised in a report in the *Korea Herald* on its 30th anniversary in 2023: J. He-rim, "Samsung's iconic Frankfurt declaration marks 30th anniversary", *Korea Herald* (June 6th 2023).

6. P. Polman, "How Much Do You Care?", LinkedIn.com (November 5th 2021). Excerpt from P. Polman and A. Winston, *Net Positive: How Courageous Companies Thrive by Giving More Than They Take* (Harvard Business Review Press, 2022).

7. P. Lencioni, *The Five Dysfunctions of a Team: A Leadership Fable* (Wiley, 2002).

Chapter 7. More effective teamwork

1. "Mission Highlights", Apollo 13: Mission Details, NASA (July 8th 2009). www.nasa.gov/missions/apollo/apollo-13-mission-details/

2. The phrase "Failure is not an option" is often falsely attributed to the NASA flight director Gene Krantz. In fact it was created as a tagline for the 1995 film *Apollo 13* and was spoken by the character who portrayed Gene Krantz. See "Origin of Apollo 13 quote: 'Failure is not an option'", spaceacts.com

3. Netflix writes extensively about its culture and the importance of collaboration, honesty, communication and how it empowers their team here: "Netflix culture – seeking excellence". jobs.netflix.com/culture

Chapter 8. Trust-based business development

1. C.M. Christenson, *The Innovator's Dilemma: The Revolutionary Book That Will Change the Way You Do Business* (HarperCollins, 2011).

2. "How trust in your organization can drive performance", Deloitte.

Chapter 9. Building trust with suppliers

1. As told to the authors by Phillip King, then the UK's Interim Small Business Commissioner, March 2020.
2. This article sets this out in more detail: D. Gelles, "Billionaire no more: Patagonia founder gives away the company", *New York Times* (September 14th 2022).
3. For a fuller description of this see "Working with factories", patagonia.com/gb/en/our-footprint/working-with-factories.html
4. C. Conn, "I want to live in a world where companies say what they are about – and act on it", Edelman (2022). www.edelman.com/trust/edelman-trust-institute/publication-2022/
5. For a full analysis, see L. Robertson, "How ethical is Nike?", Good on You (July 23rd 2023). goodonyou.eco/how-ethical-is-nike/
6. International Trade Union Confederation, "Scandal: inside the global supply chains of 50 top companies", ITUC Frontlines Report 2016.
7. "Business ecosystems come of age", *Business Trends* report (Deloitte University Press, 2015).
8. A more detailed analysis of ARM can be found in A. De Meyer and P.J Williamson, *Ecosystem Edge: Sustaining Competitiveness in the Face of Disruption* (Stanford Business Books, 2020).
9. H. Radojev, "Analysis: how Morrisons blazed a grocery trail through the Covid crisis", *Retail Week* (March 11th 2021).
10. Meyer and Williamson, *Ecosystem Edge*.

Chapter 10. Conversations that build trust

1. B. Brown, *Dare to Lead: Brave Work, Tough Conversations, Whole Hearts* (Vermilion, 2018).

Index